Mysteries of
Small Houses

Also by Alice Notley

Mysteries of
Small Houses

ALICE NOTLEY

PENGUIN POETS

PENGUIN BOOKS
Published by the Penguin Group
Penguin Group (USA) Inc., 375 Hudson Street, New York, New York 10014, U.S.A.
Penguin Group (Canada), 10 Alcorn Avenue, Toronto,
   Ontario, Canada M4V 3B2 (a division of Pearson Penguin Canada Inc.)
Penguin Books Ltd, 80 Strand, London WC2R 0RL, England
Penguin Ireland, 25 St Stephen's Green, Dublin 2, Ireland (a division of Penguin Books Ltd)
Penguin Group (Australia), 250 Camberwell Road, Camberwell,
   Victoria 3124, Australia (a division of Pearson Australia Group Pty Ltd)
Penguin Books India Pvt Ltd, 11 Community Centre, Panchsheel Park, New Delhi – 110 017, India
Penguin Group (NZ), cnr Airborne and Rosedale Roads,
   Albany, Auckland, New Zealand (a division of Pearson New Zealand Ltd)
Penguin Books (South Africa) (Pty) Ltd, 24 Sturdee Avenue,
   Rosebank, Johannesburg 2196, South Africa

Penguin Books Ltd, Registered Offices: 80 Strand, London WC2R 0RL, England

First published in Penguin Books 1998

Page vii constitutes an extension of this copyright page.

LIBRARY OF CONGRESS CATALOGING-IN-PUBLICATION DATA
Notley, Alice, 1945–
Mysteries of small houses / Alice Notley.
p.   cm. — (Penguin poets)
ISBN 0 14 058896 5 (pbk.)
I. Title.
PS3564.079M97 1998
811'.54—dc21   97-42195

Set in Perpetua
Designed by Claire O'Keeffe

146086900

*For all these people and times
and for Peggy DeCoursey,
whose constancy and support
have mattered for so many of us.*

Acknowledgments

Some of these poems have appeared in the following publications:
The American Poetry Review, Prosodia, The World, Talisman,
Bombay Gin, Fourteen Hills: The SFSU Review, Pharos, GAS,
Columbia Poetry Review, Ink Feathers, PsaLm 151, Printed
Matter, New American Writing, $lavery—Cyberzine of the
Arts, Proliferation, etruscan reader VII, The Poet's Voice,
The Chicago Review, apex of the M, *and the anthology* Best
American Poetry of 1996 *(edited by Adrienne Rich).*

Contents

Mysteries of
Small Houses

Would Want to Be in My Wildlife

hold pen improperly against 4th finger not 3rd like when I was six why won't I
hold it right

if I'm even younger four I walk more solemnly walking's relatively new but
talking's even more natural and I can see you really while we talk

if words are a sense in motion the universe has always had it

I'm not sounding young

though holding the pen wrong

I don't have to sound young but I couldn't say "oil well" right

erase all that it's not right. You have to erase whatever it is and erase before
that and before that to be perfect

no   perfect's here from ever all along and if it doesn't say it right it's right and I
am it from then now Alley House I am

and get scared till I *am* I

scareder and scareder

then calm and enter where oil of I does flow

oleanders ah touch and steps up aha oleanders oleanders and touched they make
me be here in the strange scented present

up and if I enter I have truly to enter

stars weren't alive before me anyone's from the most ancient wildness

that part's blue floor that part's pink floor kitchen washroom bathroom
backporch all small

it doesn't matter what happens here what matters is not to lose judiciousness
which wildness has from before its befores human wildness does it isn't self-deceiving
like cruelty but's unbrokenup into the parts of the bad

that's why the house is so small and I am so simple because one thing seeing and
being's the one thing there is though each one's it and though each one's different both
at least from the beginning socialization's what makes us the same in the made-up
way

House of Self

1

Back in child house
because suddenly in   Think of peachpit
Can't move arms right   too jerky
if I'm this far in

What's on shelf can of peaches label coming off
Where or what was I once
Because I'm hot now   It's bright
waterdrops are blown off the desert cooler

Cool down, night, dark
Staring at the ceiling
This neutrality of being is hard to describe
Pink their bedroom blue mine

And in the dark core that?
a black peach
with a black peachpit
House breathes around it walls respire

I'm my real body
Black peach breaks open
It's fallen it's ripe
"P" is for prognosticate

2

Sit quietly on the steps outside
in shorts
& bare-midriff top I'm skinny
the wading pool's empty

there's a big moon
over the Desert Inn Motel
the wall across the alley
with its two rows of windows

———

I'm now who I'll be, as I say, but
there's something, therefore,
lost to me
Margaret's the baby but she

already doesn't have it
well we have it but it won't come "up"
Oh—tight—it won't be us
I'm waiting

Now I can go inside   & it's dark there's
no light at all
I'm lying in my bed
in the back of the house

I well up, not telling
if I die in this wave there is no such thing
as dying, because
there's this wave, or surge and not

so powerful, except for
as much as needed
all that I am, as
much as that

3
Still empty morning house
inside
inside
there's a cool room for washing, with
        deep sinks.
Stand in here a minute
                        Outside
the sky's really plain, as usual

now go into the living room
sit down on the floor
in position opposite to cross-legged
calves splayed out from knees

———

Will there be
more grace arriving, which
won't come on call,
from inside the rafters and floor

just wait, do that, wait
because nothing's what people say
and not grace either
not what we are

it's quiet, & destructive: won't let you have
anything
no house in beauty or power
just my self

I am
what I asked for
I'm speaking
I speak like this.

I'm Just Rigid Enough

It's because I'm the same then that I'm writing this

I mean now and if we go out for a ride in the 50's car
    it's our Chevy
And I'm the one who already knows what I learn
The minute I'm shown the words——clock, hat, Bill, Susan,
"A Flaming Meteor Hits the Earth"
We ride out towards Topock I lie in the backseat
Night, somewhere after the Five-Mile Station
Against hills flowing they cry out, "Did you see that? It
    lit up the whole sky"
I'm afraid to look when I do it's gone
A week later they have *Life* magazine
"That's what we saw" on the cover a fireball
With caption "A Flaming Meteor Hits the Earth"
So I read those words, '49 or '50.

I didn't read a couple of years before, wasn't doing that
I talked when the words came but first the world
Was my recognition my just-prior knowledge of it
I'm still here in the backseat
"A Flaming Meteor Hits the Earth" contains no car or terror
How did I get to be born. And recognize the events
    of my life
Some of them were always going to be
But I don't want any events——I have, even early, revulsion
    for their names:
Graduation, marriage, childbirth
The meteor's named by science
We name us and then we are lost, tamed
I choose words, more words, to cure the tameness, not the wildness.

I remember everything it isn't past it's wild
I'm so constant and have nearly lost myself only seldom, later,
But *I* would have lost it, lost me
Flaming Meteor I was scared of you first
I love this alley, love is recognition
Born in love.

Kiss of Fire

Walk out onto playground
Fenced-in blacktop extends into desert
towards Seven Mile Mountains, no shade
one is not yet socially de-
formed—impression of kindness of mutual
interest, of equality· We the kids think we're equal
a long while after we've been judged
dissimilar in intellect.
I discover being funny
parodying a torch singer
a girl leads me about, like my agent, at lunchtime
to perform my version of "Kiss of Fire"
"Listen to this," she says—between tar and the sun
I touch your lips and all
at once the sparks go flying, those devil
lips that know so well the art of lying
heat, in heat who, in isolation who
will ever leave town and kiss a liar
Everyone's transparent here, one is thoroughly known

and if you left town and kissed a liar
that would be somewhat trivial abandoning
the unkissable desert the netherworldly mountains—
they already signify death—
in order to be lost in manners, as I will be
so I can sing. I know I must surrender to
your kiss of fire. We play in the sun.
After school in the gully, where I
first heard the word "fuck" spoken, ess-shaped
snake chasm of the world. Eerie
eerie you might stay and
become Gravel Gertie, bag lady in a gully
out by the dump   because she does life all by her-
self, and she only talks to dogs and to the
desert. And only the desert is real; and if

I ever leave town, that will be
wonderful but it won't be the real real.
Just like a torch within my soul within me
burning, I must go on and on and on with no
returning   and then something about ashes and crashes,
If I'm a slave then it's a slave I want to be,
don't pity me   Adults seem to have no irony
Somewhere on a road, where the climate begins to change,
a couple of poplar trees, but that's no shade.

One of the Longest Times

My brother's always in the gully
Too ugly for me down there
But in the vacant lot next to the house
I pile towels on a creosote bush in the corner
We all go in and sit
Does it smell like creosote oil and have flowers like stars

Albert Margaret and me, holding sacred things here
Sticks and rocks
Small black-scored rock is
The quantum life-story object, take it
Life's beginning and over compact in your dirty palm

We're huddled in here don't need anyone we're
Star-sent-out light that's still alive
We're still here sending out us
As stars from the first world melt
Why aren't we the same as each other
Rocks look the same I'll never be you

This rock's me from before the flood and after the fire
This rock's you and what happens to you it adds up to
This rock this time and
This time in this bush is long, long
Becky's our baby our sister and this one
Is hers from before the flood
And after the fire that comes
I am a rock in these shadows who
Am I speaking to who am I speaking

I got this me. This one's you. What's the point
It would be better if
We all died together

We put and put rocks; I have life coming (life's
Nothing but THIS minute
Something for you a brown stick for you)

This is the longest one of the longest times
It lasts after we're dead and after all people
Are dead; how do you know
Because thoughts have lasted since the first thought
'Cause I think that we're in the first thoughts still
Lasting and we last
And we last, making real selves

The Future May Contain Me More

I'm at the Needles Civic Center
across from the tracks and train station
and there's Mohave Park looking dried-out
I walk up the stairs past the jail
into the single room dark, dark wood all around.

Straight ahead near her desk
are the Junior Books I've read those—
Anne of Avonlea, Sue Barton, R.N ; I started out
with Vicki Barr, Airline Stewardess.
I'm still fascinated by a plot in a Vicki Barr book:
Vicki Barr knows a girl with a scar on her face
whose problems she cures with a makeup product
applied to the center of the scar then spread carefully outward.
The girl has a designer scarf—and actually knows the designer—
blue with silver bells. The girl now looks beautiful in it
she will teach her rival who has the scarf
in a less personally becoming red with gold bells
how to tie the scarf, as the designer taught her,
so that the bells show to their best advantage.

This story's pleasing to consider but I'm older
it's a childish geometrical proof but now
I need older books. G.B. Shaw is famous
I've read some of his prefaces and plays—I wonder why
I can understand them. There's the sexy book *Kathryn*
about John of Gaunt's mistress Kathryn Swynford
redhaired and bigbreasted golden, not like dead delicate Blanche
Chaucer's a minor character; I'll read his poetry later
I'm way down the left wall looking—this
book looks interesting, woman in Shakespeare's times,
becomes lover of Christopher Marlowe—who's he?
I think I'll also reread this book by Anya Seton about
a Puritan's tortured daughter, John Winthrop's daughter Elizabeth
whose illicit lover calls her Hinny, not Honey, Hinny Sweet.

Outside again I walk to the drugstore call Momma to
get a ride home from the book rack and soda fountain the shelves of
dusting powder Why can't we use Yardley's soap especially
the crushed carnation scent? Because it's
too expensive a dollar fifty for box of three. There's
Old Spice for men, but Daddy doesn't use his;
Kathy's father uses something I associate with the word Jade.

It's hot outside in the wind, in the bottle
we live in that fills the whole world—if I don't
get to leave time stops that's all, it's already
stopped for a long time. I'm too old for the Jane Eyre
Classics Comic back in there; I've read the book itself now
several times. I don't want to look at her anyway
she's all brown except for gray sky;
I'm sort of like that too, brown but not gray, faded blue.

Synchronous Chronology

To estrus and estrogen very responsive
be her, barefoot sixteen-year-old
I won't be different in the future
I won't ever change

body length breasts pressed to air of a quadrillion pieces
of blankness potential to hierophany
she's standing like a ghost in my Paris apartment
she's a flawless young human body——my past me

able bend of morning the light'd sway down
but not close and broad like later in the day not hot
clothes are compact and uncomplex
she's walking to school after breakfast
she washes her hair twice a week
beauty in art is eternal, music enlightenment

there is a soul that she is but delicately fainter
shadows cover it, layers
of words, it can't compete with
lipstick smear
of isolate kisses still immune to the future

Can you woo your own soul, but what else am I?
in my Paris room
I'm showing that girl that I'm it
she nods gravely has had time to figure
I may have wanted better for her
in terms of the transparent good——giving self easily
to strangers——but

she protected me, for example, from
the Job's Daughters
their Masonic idiocy in white vestal robes
and she didn't hate anyone, not for a long time

---

who is she really, falls away further
I am hierophanic in the blue air there of the past
I give you myself protect me and you'll have a later
protect me, change, but defend me
singular image

The Obnoxious Truth

Inside this little theater
inside the high school auditorium (new) there is a stage on which.
(A small room I'm now allowed fame in) in a blue chiffon dress
      playing Debussy
make mistakes, nobody knows—not even the man who says that
I'm not good enough to be a writer, should be a musician.

It's of no interest to be here now

partly because I can't tell them I'm not good enough. (won't let me
They want me to put one over on them)
I'm trying to think but I'm dreaming; under the roof
I'm trying to think
about what a life is not triumphant sex
I want to go away where I can't do some things as well as others do—
I want my abilities to be clear
at least I'll be made to think there—won't I—the true thoughts.

To be in the true thoughts you must forget
possessions, of course, I don't want them anyway
looks except as expression of good feelings
sex except as it happens
talent except as it performs without causing envy
run the risk of being the only person around who's scrupulous
they hate you, they make fun of me actually
they like me but they patronize what will be known in ignorance as
      my "idealism."

Can you be how you want despite others, I hope to (still)
I'll always be this adolescent—I'm right that I won't change
I may seem insufferable to you, I want to live in true thoughts
this desert with nothing between me and it never trembles
such clarity obviates the heart
the kind that smothers the world in productions
but not the kind heart that thinks and not only in words.

Am I back onstage, Arabesque No. 1 done, they're going to
praise me again, but I didn't play it right.
Look at these gold lamé shoes, look at my hair

Requiem for the First Half of Split

An early sadness for the future
(as in dreams of myself young and sad)
accompanies my departure towards
a conventional story· a town
of girls a New York City dormitory
And so a trail proceeds from
our house on the top of the hill
down the back way of former army barracks
and past the borrowed church (ours had no tank)
where I was baptized
reasoning "it must be true" out of
the love I had for my mother
And Tony's house there across the street from it
absolutely in the Mexican gully
in dreams of which he and I still fight armed enemies
he stepped on a land mine in Nam
when I remind my brother, twenty years after
his face contorts he knows the look of that death
a week before he himself dies
blood-tinged ruddy-winged, but that's another
dream-site the Needles Cemetery inelegant
unbeautiful and dear and dry
See how many loves, how much thus sadness
in the future begins to
haunt that walk down that hill
towards the highway away to the dormitory
as I go to New York to sever love's connections
and make the "real ones" generated by
actual mating by beauty and clothes
the black wool suit with its three button jacket
the oddly puffed-sleeved orange sweater
and an orange and midnight-
blue paisley waistless dress.
New trail there,
Brett knows my future love though I don't

hitchhikes with him to California
years before I catch up to the poets in Iowa City
that will be in '69, my brother
hasn't yet signed up for Nam then
when he gives me rattles off a rattler
which I keep in my wooden India box I still have
until they stink.
I can't keep track of the track there's nothing but
sidetrails of love and sadness so love is
all that makes my people act they go to war for love
you know, of who and what you are
like I was baptized by
the cruellest-lipped prissiest-mouthed man in the world
for love, but I could just have gone swimming
walked back up love's hill
back up at the house you can get to the pool
barefoot if you can find enough
bush or telephone-pole shadows.
We'd all swim together
I'd tread water dreaming of the future
but a wilder larger eye birdlike
distant holds the pool in its pupil
anyone's that too, and hold the enlarging
water sad how not be
why don't the smart girls in New York know this
why don't you or I know what we know
the eye and the water both enlarge still why don't
smart girls in Paris, yes larger but will never flood
the containing eye, but why not
and sometimes it does
when you or your own are the news.

Experience

In the mountains of New York
he was my first savior jack of clubs
though one's divided between
if he tells you or you tell yourself—
you know what I mean?—
what's true.
Waiting in rooms full of girls.
An older man does the trick
Not as dumb as a younger one, but
they fuck without compunction at
first then they get some because
you're too dumb.
He was tall greeneyed person
pale with features disappearing
into that paleness apartment on Hudson St.
the rest is a secret no it isn't
Why no secrets? Oh,
who reads poetry anyway!
I can almost see green sweater
a peculiarly vegetative
moss or heatherish green
gets unbuttoned, bare bulb light.
He's too dumb to think I'm innocent
what kind of stupidity's operative
this man's a doctor I
scream he's surprised a hymen bleeds.
After that I'm a lump of naiveté
to him in every respect and so
discarded I now have experience.
I think this kind of tale is
as important as a pompously cited
Phoenician myth, to poetry
in Phoenix I drink with my father
"You don't bruise the bourbon," he says.
Back in New York, uptown at night

a warehouse city no street life
Rooms full of girls I'll always dream about
Women won't let me go Or is it men
A sex isn't very deep but its
surface is armor ironmasked
like certain poetries I can't use
how be what you are what's experience but
a becoming acceptable to the keepers
of surfaces say this University
So glad I don't have to write
in the styles of the poetries I was taught
they were beautiful and unlike me
positing a formal, stylized woman.
But I am the poet, without doubt.
Experience is a hoax.

1965

I'll give you what I know if you'll
give too
of course I'll go as far towards
world as supposed to I'm
a good girl
though I won't lose my darkness what
else do I have
sit in it on a dead tomb of knowing
turn out light to lie down on girl tomb knowing
everyone else in the gold net of being
college Upper Broadway New York
busy handing me pieces of delicately
iced over words past beauty's breath or
soldier books
trees in the yard transparently encased from
an ice storm end of January
I'd like to call up my lover
but he isn't he hates me
so my folksong's really
working which fact I don't know
I'm miserable because I'll die someday
blond girl who's wild points out loveliness of trees
because she thinks I'm interesting too but no one's
what anyone thinks
if I return to the desert I'll die there
want the secrets of culture not realizing
I now am them am it hurt others
every step I take with the having of
this prize I'll never go
back on
the trees make glass clicks blown gently
but if there's delicacy to be cultivated did I

learn it in privilege so that I could touch
cold words together and make a sound of a girl
who was colder than I knew
perhaps still is

Prophet's Job

620 West 116th St school housing apartment girls
there's a kitchen but I don't cook. They broil an occasional
thigh I remember it blond naked sprinkled with herbs
it's Susan she's engaged, everyone wants to be.
Not me, I'd prefer to be upset by boyfriend but not
in a motion towards permanent coupling, rather
in a motion towards understanding feelings, I've a print
a detail from the Eisenheim Altarpiece on my wall a fiery-
haired pointy-haired angel grinning and playing a viol
to remind me to wait for epiphany I've had the first
of my negative epiphanies—my first fear of
dying overwhelming my whole second year there but not
as grotesque as when, in Iowa City some three
years later, I'll fear each night the materialization
of a ghost I never see. Why don't I understand these
fears are the same as the mystic's joy they're as
intense and as much a show of divinity the strength of
my emotion commensurate with that of what creates us,
so I've only the one picture there that femaleish
spirit of music and saturated hues, green vermilion and gold.
How much do I wish angelic possession and not a boyfriend
who wants a profession and to be husbanded to
a sweet-faced girl. In the future I'll dream I
insult Susan accuse her of wealth, a rash on her face
which changes mild brown eyes grow unhappy I accuse you
of money, am I wrong to hurt you individually ór
if I could hurt more individuals so in my poems
wouldn't I be doing my strange job better
Now young I think scarcely of wealth I've no time
I'm full of the wish to survive nights like this
where in doubt of his feelings for me I leave Susan
eating her thigh I lie down in the dark at 8 o'clock

on Saturday night, waiting to change from despair to calm
that takes all night, there will be other times
when it will take years I suspect. If only the angel
but negative feelings fear and despair are my angel.

As Good as Anything

I don't see the point of
remembering you; you're too boring,
Iowa City, Iowa,
much duller topologically than
Needles, California. I'm here
in the Rebel Motel, with
my grape-colored sweater
and maté tea, whose smoky odor's
bound up with first rooms and foods here
sex and snow I
write about Needles
Herman and rocks, the story's called
"As Good as Anything," and in it
daft Herman—true local
of Needles—says
"Rocks is as good as anything."
I figured that out summer after
first love affair in New York:
hung out, home, at a rock shop
inspecting geodes and thunder eggs
Arsenic samples and petrified
dinosaur dung.
What can I say about Iowa City
everyone's an academic poetry
groupie, I haven't yet written a poem,
there's a bar where for 25 cents a
meal of boiled egg and tiny beer
Really I don't know what kind of poetry---
what's the name of the make they
use here—or what kinds of
poetry live people write in the world.
Is there a right and wrong poetry, one might
still ask as I patronize,
retrospectively, the Iowa style,
characterized, as I remember,

by the assumption of desperation
boredom behind two-story houses
divorce, incomes, fields, pigs,
getting into pants, well not really
in poems, well no "well"s and all
in the costive mode
of men who——and the suicidal women——
want to be culpable for something,
settle for being mean to their wives
and writing dour stanzas. God this is bitchy
I modeled for art classes
that's rather interesting
the hypocrisy· nobody *needs*
to paint nude women
they just like to. So here I am
naked for art, which is a lot of
dumb fucks I already know,
same with poetry
Written and judged by Those befoibled guys
who think——you know——
the poetic moment's a pocket in
pool; where can I publish it; what can
I do to my second or third wife now
Nothing happens in Iowa, so
can I myself change here? Yes
I can start to become contemptuous
is that good or bad, probably bad.
In New York I'd developed a philosophy
of sympathy and spiritual equality·
out the window, easily, upon
my first meeting real assholes.
"A rock's as good as anything"
there are no rocks in Iowa
shit-black soil, a tree or two,
no mountain or tall edifice,
University drabs, peeping Toms, anti-war
riots, visiting poets
treated like royalty, especially if

they fuck the locals or have a record
of fighting colorfully with their wives.
You can go to the movies once a week,
like in Needles. You can fuck
a visiting poet; you can be paraded before
a visiting poet as fuckable but not fuck.
You can write your first poems
thinking you might as well
since the most stupid people in the universe
are writing their five hundredth here.
I'm doing that now What
difference does it make.
I like my poems. They're
as good as rocks.

"Go In and Out the Window"

In the great American
poem anything
can't you, can't you
not be an
American be an in and out of
species even tongue of grass or fire and not the
shit in our sinking cesspool behind alley house
Momma and Charley stand in '49 or '50
and look at the collapsing lawn
contains everything everyone thinks needs
to go into a poem, the history of
anything all the information edification
theoreticals opinions showings off your
teacher told you would make your
name,

the poem is not your name.
"Go in and out" the purple Chinaberry blossom spring
air, the poison oleander fragility frontyard
It's a bubble, poem air bubble   not
from people shooting up, "fixing" M called it
to be more or less of self
like the speedfreak suicide sometime after
I left the Marrakech house
I'd found hippie life boring vacuous due to
lack of poetry, we'd brought nothing
to let us pass in and out the black and star sky over the
red clay and green palm medina.

Where's your poem Alice?
                    Here it is but
not mine, I
want it but have to go in order for it to live
or go in and out, I go in and out
of it "and see what we can see"

part of me
is, I'm finding at 23 Iowa Spain Morocco
in 1968, a pinpoint of social ego so
why, I don't know, the only
time I've ever been paranoid
on strong hash in the Marrakech house I'm
attacked by paranoia as an
outer force
as if we all together create disembodied madnesses
in the same way as we extrude
other kinds of shit

I leave the room to find an orange
crave something bright and succulent so I
won't have to be
the word "paranoid"
won't have to be a hippie on hash
American poet of this or that possession
American woman in a mini with black tights
fresh from whatever shit repository,
somebody else's person
                              I go in and out, in '94
slide away in mind, walk across the Grand Souk
or the lot next to the alley house,
know how to do
that now losing useless info like
stardust, sparkles emitted from head
electric tracings of socialization
There's nothing in that woman's brain out the window—
she couldn't write a poem--who is she, Momma? is she
me? She doesn't know anything.

April Not an Inventory but a Blizzard

I met Ted at two parties at the same house
at the first he insulted me because, he said later,
he was mad at girls that night; at the second we danced
an elaborate fox-trot with dipping—he had once taken one lesson
at an Arthur Murray's. First I went into an empty
room and waited for him to follow me. I liked the way
his poems looked on the page open but delicately arranged.

I like him because he's funny he talks more like
me than like books or words: he likes my knowledge and
accepts its sources. I know that there are Channel swimmers
and that they keep warm with grease because of
an Esther Williams movie. We differ as to what kind
of grease it is I suggest bacon he says it's bear
really in the movie it was dark brown like grease from a car
Who's ever greased a car? Not him I find he prefers to white out
all the speech balloons in a Tarzan comic
and print in new words for the characters. Do you want
to do some? he says—No—We go to a movie where Raquel Welch
and Jim Brown are Mexican revolutionaries I make him
laugh he says something about a turning point in the plot
Do you mean, I say, when she said We shood have keeled him long ago?
Finally a man knows that I'm being funny

He's eleven years older than me and takes pills
I take some a few months later and write
I think it's eighty-three poems I forget about Plath and James Wright
he warns me about pills in a slantwise way See this
nose? he says, It's the ruins of civilization
I notice some broken capillaries who cares

I wonder who I am now myself though I haven't
anticipated me entirely I have such an appetite
to write not to live I'm certainly living quite fully
We're good together he says because we can be like

little boy and little girl I give him much later a
girl's cheap Dutch brooch Delft blue and white
a girl and a boy holding hands and windmills
But now it's summer in Iowa City he leaves for
Europe gives me the key to his library stored
in a room at The Writers Workshop
I write mildly yet oh there's a phrase "the Gilbert curve"
how a street turns that sensation to make it permanent
a daily transition as the curve opens and is walked on
of the kinds of experience still in between the ones
talked about in literature and even in Ted's library
which finally makes poetry possible for me but I've
not read a voice like my own like my own voice will be

1970

I want to put it in code can't find one
this light has no gloss it's a shabby wall.
After a few weeks together on the
West Coast and a temporary parting
to separate states practicalities
Ted will come by car to move with me to
New York: he says but doesn't I wait no
word someone tells me he's in New York
already and living with a woman
twenty-four years ago but I can still
dream this faithlessness freshly last night
context of lordly storefront hippies.
Someone's free to do this to me I am
free or unfree to be hurt as deeply
as dreams but not as deeply as art for
when I write I don't care what else is. I
go to his city where else be a poet
world of vintage dresses vests and pills like
refractive crystal buttons against dark
velvet or flat like stars on a headband.
Mature when youngest we grow up to be
children we people who're brilliant treat each
other like conquests or allies earrings
worn until discarded bloody clip-on
roses I mean wear them wear me he does
it to me with her then later we do
it to her in a group of many poets
and artists all in changeable coupling
formations so I can't believe I'm loved.
Does it matter who for him I'm here but
friable and he might do anything
inflected by a broken marriage and no
nobility or luster to my love
which is fanatical from hurt. How did
I become one seemingly who gives whole

self away on a whim this obscurant
relationship will become lambent in
the years of our marriage but breaking my-
self now for sex is not what I'd predict
from my future or my earliest past.
Nothing deep in me makes me be like that
I'm not that possession I enact it
but it comes from the world where Eros was
invented how am I happy at the
same time as not I love and write alive.

Choosing Styles——1972

I thought of words breaking open in the mouth but
also as jewels
of old sexless poets, of the dead dessicated
except for those emeralds or topazes
I still get a thrill when I say, emeralds and topazes.
Who wants to say "freightage," what is the charge for that word
who wants to say "distress" and wear the black chiffon
scarf inside it
who wants to write in old long lines clearly and not be
slightly more inscrutable
askance in freaker
lines, in brilliance
outflame
blaze; flash——
Chose sometimes more for beauty or for clarity
or for some arbitrary reason——no reason I know go
against word order· firstling you
by dint of me, clean, sings up in the clerestory
of the donned doom show Worthless filmy daughterous
contagion in the durable shell
take the horse nearest the door——
maybe that's what I really did, chose, and the other side's
hissing,
hissing.
There are these sides I'm tired of it
Float in air liaison with illicit spirit
Who cares how I write?
Okay Pained and similar plants, now don't I have to
give? The poem will tell you its secret light-of-hand
that everyone will die before
any knows which way to write right
mouthmouthed I mean foulmouthed motherfucking turds you are
shit in the wind, frail shit blown back, because I
am onstage. Ah, frag you John. Glisten and twisted fingers
into unmouthed ruby of glum blood we'll go,

doing what with our digits——counting the gloaming light
in anyone's glass legend coursing through them
one glob two globs rounded mass of wishful self is in
these tiny red boxing glove particles, these
ultimate pieces of identity, which permeate
any poor matter's glee and grief. I forgot: My style is to
forget whence we came; the origins of
my style. I'm gnarling at you.
Moon and underworld, queen and cunt where the molten
metal flows. My style comes from death.
A jinni, a power, I don't have to care
how I write, in what manner——up-to-date *are you
kidding*? You're dead!
Menstruation covered with sand, garnets and amber

Not Child

Can't today am not
in the childhood black house my
life's unhinged and blowing round me
clouds and tatters
Sold a car this day in Chicago
for 25$ to one Tom Grub
I can't even drive, pregnant I
will be miserable in this house
black crow death flap left shoulder
Ted saw his first ghost here
I saw my own, Goodbye good
girl, phone ringing and ringing
she's calling me up she
wants me to stay unsocially pure; but I
have sullied her
with living around people, ab-
sorbing their oh so
definite ideas of how to proceed
write be female
mother and dress, what's a girl's joke- -
do women have wit
Take a crash course
in a prescribed humor Later take a
crash course in
sorrow, "You aren't funny
like you used to be."
You ain't pretty you ain't funny
you ain't as famous as you shoulda been
huge wind clouds blow the stained glass in
Glue the pane back together?
"We were, are so brilliant." Well
I don't know about that.
What have we made but
difficulty, a species which can't
laugh and play like god, can only

prevaricate   predominate   prefer?
This house
is big and lonely—like starting
all over in Paris
twenty years later; people still saying
Frank O'Hara's no good—
Eliot alive in the hospital,
or turn the corner and find some
fin-de-siècle non-referentiality· but
what about the planet itself?
Open the fortune cookie:
"You will regret when the ruby breaks
that you staked your life on the intrigues
of a sub-group of mammals
who worshiped the dust in their eyes."
Bad I've been bad in this house
I've allowed burning inside me; I
remember my ancient dream,
in which a woman tells me,
"Your house only burns *inside*; it's
still standing   " Some consolation,
an internal firestorm.
all I do is make thought.
Chicago or Paris, am I? New York,
San Francisco
Where's the most distorted being
I've ever been?

A Baby Is Born Out of a White Owl's Forehead—1972

At this time there are few
poems about pregnancy and childbirth
do I find this curious
I want to shriek at
any identity
this culture gives me claw it to
pieces; has nothing to
do with me or
my baby and never will,
has never perceived a
human being.
My baby is quiet and wise, but I'm
a trade name and I'm
chaos
rainwater on a piano—I'm so
scared then but now of then I'd say
I want to make your tunes go away
to have a child is more casual
than, you might say, and more serious than
the definition
for who, frankly, was ever born
or gave birth?

After the usual pain and the well-meaning,
mostly but not all,
intervention of others and others' words and meanings
I find him. Lying next to me yes and being
nursed by me.
I serve him why not he isn't wrong.

I'm infused with a noxious dispirit
as the world makes me be a woman
everything has gone wrong in some sense by now

Of two poems one sentimental and one not
I choose both
of his birth and my painful unbirth I choose both.
The woman in the photo has a haircut from Vidal Sassoon
wears a black silky synthetic top and probably a long skirt
the baby on her lap in sleepers and
a blue and white Peruvian cap.
They look abstracted in the same way
He is the baby unchaotic
he is born and I am undone—feel as if I will
never be, was never born.

Two years later I obliterate myself again
having another child
not to be a form of woman
but in allegiance to the process I
can't quite see.
I have begun to be.

I sit with my sons in a barely cared-for apartment
inside from Chicago in the TV's ambience (black and
white, like the snow) purple crocuses there
Ted's becoming sick with a lasting illness
though we are calm while money doesn't press us
a moment of happiness, these bodies are clear
all four finally clear and
still clear

but first, for two years, there's no me here.

They Cut Out Her Eye and So
She Doesn't Know If It's Real

I remember a year I was
afraid all the time
the overall taste was iron
interiors of somber
glissade in a large house, shaken and
falling quite
literally

Fell down afraid to get up
Afraid of my body
its dizziness created its
brain's rush of fear-thought My
real self seemed buried
the house was its tomb
light a war to
walk fearlessly
darkness was possible
possession

Afraid of movies and books
Open to all their quackery I'd
seen a ghoulish movie
and changed
charged with fear
like a child and read a book
which said Death sits
your death sits
upon your left shoulder and then
crow's wings were there
closed the book didn't finish

in those days art could be dangerous

No this was real fear

any drama can be made absurd but
this was fear of death of dying and
most of all loss of
my true self
in monstrousness suicide or
violence death of others
by my hand   My
brother's fate after all was
to kill and isn't it really
your hand
You kill in your country's wars with
your possessions   your clothes and
cars kill your
food kills
you back you have always backed your
economy

I had above my desk another's
beautiful
poem about fear
about having once been brave
being fearful
I'd become so much other
was later purged but
not of my self I
was purged of un-
reality the
delusion of a placid life amid
American things as
mental arrangement a person of
her times I don't
believe in my times and their invidious
forms of art their shallow
castings about for
meaning
without one's giving up so much as
an inch
of skin

or finding a voice to speak in
not a voicelessness
scramble of fear   *fear* of the self
because it isn't
like us
as we've
become   would have to wrench so much
away
and so we deny it and sink
with fear
to the floor at its least
vibration

Diversey Street

I'm in a house that's too big
the Diversey St. house
Ted sees a ghost a young girl
cross the kitchen and disappear
through the door that leads upstairs
I don't exactly believe that or
maybe I believe I'm the
ghost myself, asleep, and
awake at the same time
haunting my house. I see two
pieces of shattered glass full of light
you and I sleeping. Climb down in the dark
down into the basement or
up where the guests might lie.
Only walk free, only released
from fear in my sleep.

Aureoles of lamps are too bright, awake.
I've written a failed poem of lilacs.
Can I ever forgive myself for my thoughts,
for my fear of a crazed demise?
In this pointlessness of modern
physicality, this body, admired house.

And then someone says,
I think you should write happier poems.
More than once I'm asked to deny
my experience.
The weight of this house's shadows.
I'm so in it now
As a ghost I am perhaps from the future.
Ghost in an own life of mine.
Because fear blocks the door
And can't I bring the baby to the future.
I can't believe the future comes

except as tragedy
I let smug men say things about my poems.
Am I trying to turn into
a smug man so I—fear sits on I
so I won't be afraid, I guess.

And deeper still
who's afraid. Is it I.
Below who's afraid's the one who isn't.
The ghost from the future. I almost
believe I will prevail
when I'm asleep and the future
haunts this house.

I Must Have Called and So He Comes

"You're accusing me of something in these poems."
"No Ted, I'm not accusing you—can't catch your voice though."
"Through dead curtains," he says. Gives me the disgusted
   Berrigan moue, casts match aside lighting cigarette
"So what are you doing?" he says. I say, "As the giant lasagne
   on Star Trek—remember, Spock mindmelds with her
   and screams, Pain." "So this is pain?" he says.
"I suppose it is. Was. But not from you," I say
"We don't say pain we say fucked-up," he says, "Or
   Kill the motherraper Inside yourself   " (he fades)
"I can't catch your voice   " (I say)
"   there's a place inside you," he says, "a poetry self, made by
         pain but not
violated—oh I don't say violated,
   you're not getting my dialogue right, you can't remember
         my style."
"Would you say touched, instead?" I say
"There's this place in us," he says, "the so-called pain can't
         get to
like a shelter behind those spices—·coffee and sugar, spices,
matches, cockroach doodoo on the kitchen shelf.
But I was exhausted from being good without pills—
went off them on Diversey you'll remember—and you were
wearing me out. Well just a little. I took pills to
keep from thinking, myself. Do something else don't think
you're a poet write a poem for chrissakes, you're not
         your thoughts;
but I was afraid   you were mad at me deep down then."
"I don't think so," I say   "Men were a problem—I
         see that better
in the future, but you, sometimes you were 'men'
usually not." "Then were men men?" he says, "I mean —"

45

"No, I'll interrupt," I say, "Someone was being those times
    why else was I unhappy " "Do you want to know," he says,
"if I loved you in 1970?" "No," I say, "I don't."
"Anything later than Chicago? But I've just got
    a minute," he says. "No that's either your business
    or something I already know," I say, "I really enjoyed the late 70's
        in New York, you know "
"You haven't wanted to talk to me since I died," he says.
"That's true," I say, "Too dangerous. But I want to say there's no
        blame here. I see your
    goodness, plainly I want to be
    clear; I'm a detachment"—"As I am obviously," he says,
    his voice getting fainter

Colors—1973

It's an English year, richly languaged and colored—
I'm still tormented, and faced with the contrast
between a garden and me; being shut out of nature
hurts me   Thought, as possession, my depression
does this to me. And so don't think just don't
a coppery beech beneath November star—and down
the street yew and holly Tiny snowdrops in December
My first crocuses push up through me, purple, yellow
I become Dante-esque, crowded with Europeanness
of rose light—later—as highest mirror, beauty's
citadel, of grace. These petals are all my fingertips
if I don't think, don't remember myself I'm not a
woman by identity though I'm pregnant and obsessed with
the Feminine. Don't believe in it it's words, I
believe in the textures I like: cream of unyellow daffs,
apricot-pink roses, grain-of-wood voices my friends have
rock garden voices like efficaceous herbs and grasses
You always wore gray, gray sweater and cords and once
stood in my kitchen first staring and then full of words:
another man making a speech at me—I'm under
pressure to speak, "But that's boring," I say;
pregnant, surely I have the right to say I'm not mad or
bored. I think you're graceful, and when I marry you
in 15 years you'll remind me of this moment in Wivenhoe.
My child in blue blaze sweater eats my own apple;
transparent red berries, Michaelmas daisies, unfamiliar
There's the sea, over there somewhere, cold black death
merciless the universe would shut me out of its
happiness, its mind isn't like mine anymore its mind is
innocent can't absorb mine, forgiving me: my negative
thoughts bounce back at me from the flowers, like colors.

Waveland (Back in Chicago)

Go into a room in '74 while the house is quiet
Cut or tear and paste, paint orange pink red and black
Use sequins, velvet, letters, careless words
Once paste on a whole white glove.
Frozen collection of world—this is "art" I don't
write much poetry;
I'm thinking with my hands —a ploy against fear —
I have a pile of garbage on the floor

Here is a collage called WATERMASTER
made from the cardboard packet for a toilet tank part
Here's a photo of a stripper I've named
Barney   surrounded by cutout words she
dances to poetry and Here's
DEFIES YOU THE RHYTHMIC FRAME, heaped with
black sequins and sticker nasturtiums
the one-line poem spelled out in stick-on gold letters.

I must be making my own universe
out of discards
It reminds me — now in '95— of my
brother's gun collection, a
museum of war in his basement
hundreds of guns knives a dart blower a delicate
Nazi butterfly knife—
war as shape, texture, design
"A poem is a machine made out of words   "

And as we participate in our various technologies
who's innocent and who isn't, if
no one is innocent in dreams?
And below dreams, the stillness of all this "art"

What is a poem   this
What is a poem in '74   it's like a

48

collage, shapes in conjunction of world and bright color
any word I think of goes, in vivacious audacious blurting—
when I write—
Do I have your feelings? I mean now
I often discovered
I did but now I don't

in '95 I would guess not.
Purify self of collage? it's become illusory
we are illusion-machine, guiltier

Black window to my right in '74
I'm making a work that's "too" something, '95
"too" discursive "too" plain?
A poem must be of its times without giving in to them
A poem must be better than its times as
a self must be—
This poem's a black window, not a collage
I'll have to bless it myself.

Collage

Sometimes just to make something
Pretty prettier than
What's around in the mind to
Dominate
So there's first the sequin red or other
Remembering favorite
Paper dolls a dress strapless
Sheath of blue sequins
At bottom a pink tulle flounce
Of course I later hated that stuff
I mean I
Like the one sparkle next to a piece of
Torn gold foil
This collage will be a ragged experience
I've never found beauty harmonious
It tears at our lack of harmony
You you are the wound
Says anyone to anyone
This infantile mob this molesting song of yours
Your individual-getting-rocks-off feeling
But in the dime store's beauty that's where and there's
Meanly a lace of no doctrine or power to tie
Around the neck or wrist or thigh
Well of course not I'm lonely tie it for who
Tie it across the sky and its expansive provincialism
Telling us the length of our eternities
Glue it to the sky of the paper
And I was narciss recess young
Poignant enough to be something that
Another element in the collage an
Arrowed green line on chewing gum wrapper
Youth was knowing before becoming then being
Interestingly hurt by becoming
So did girl know as much then when less bent as now
Being more bent and knowing

But she didn't know what I know
She's beauty and I   I don't know what am I
Add something else torn but black cloth soft
With hard and fake a yellow "topaz" the
Most beautiful thing I've ever seen
Because the best is always now and some paint my
Old gold ink
And diamondlike pieces of shattered car window
The really ruined world

"Bring Me a Pea Jacket and Sandwiches"

Young smooth face, look he's grown very young
        to die;
no glasses or mustache in intensive care.
Then unhooked from tubes to be moved from there
to a private room: that's when he asks
for his pea jacket and sandwiches for "the boat."
I smuggle Edmund in under my coat——my second
baby——because my father likes his Irish grin,
no first we have the conversation where I tell him
I have to cry and he says "That's your prerogative."
I think that remark that carven word
makes him a keeper of my words, a muse, long after
his death; he comes to me in dreams
and tells me to make things: a raft for your sons,
he says on a beach strewn with dead alligators and
        blue lapis;
"Where is my corpus sagrada?"——obviously a poem——
        he cries in another
He's deep in me and I talk to him more, cede him
a privilege for his awesome death, a position of
        authority in my
imagination. I may not be honest enough
I don't know if he talks to me, if we only had dreams
        and not speech I'd
think dreams were real. Perhaps imagination's
        a better word for mind
than mind is. Back at the hospital in '75,
he will die: we take turns sitting up all night by
his bedside——I write "Alice Ordered Me To Be Made"
there, in colored pieces of old speech.
He becomes more and more comatose, his breathing
violently hoarse and quick——I feel he's being sucked into
        a whirlwind of death.
He dies when no one's there, at the age of fifty-five
of cirrhosis of the liver, manager and part owner of Needles

Auto Supply; he certainly
supplies me with auto parts, pieces of subcutaneous self.
A few months later in Chicago, after heat's orange lilies,
Ted becomes ill with what's diagnosed as
alcohol hepatitis; perhaps he's been drinking a lot
but he hates drink so we haven't counted it. I catch
by accident a TV program on diseases of the liver·

75 percent of cases of alcohol hepatitis lead eventually
to cirrhosis." So that's the future. But in the future
I won't talk to Ted when he's dead—I must retain my
autonomy; we'd become too much of each other
And we'd said everything anyway (had we ever). The subject
of this poem is not how a woman's imagination
may be dominated by a man's. Not how a person's imagination
must allow in some others to be lively; nor is it the story
of two men close to me dying of drink.
This poem escapes and exists beyond words for me, as I do,

picturing myself now

perched, crouched, in a leafless tree at night,

looking down.

The Howling Saint T-Shirt

Children don't come from deep inside one
they were always outside and, I dream,
wear their own saint T-shirts as I do
mine's saint image is faceless, howling.
They have smiling bodies friendly asses
"Give you Everything the first seven years," Ted says
they bear no relation to your self,
not a haunt that shakes loose not seed pod
not a part of the body not you; it's harrowing
to stop being the child yourself but
"child" is not real spiritually as classification
as I change with experience lose confidence and truth
and must find out everything from them now
As I once was they're true in their separate houses:
rhythm of the ribs, iris eyes, and patter
lead me back from depression in Hades. First I'm
fearful of what's called motherhood—
I call it unpaid work like poetry—but a family
is not a fate, it's that we're nakedly related
our heirlooms are thought to be
doomed psyches that's just one myth
a psyche's not real a soul is,
a grave child that peers from his first house.
My kids are like me superficially so I watch them
or, writing, ignore them, until they say something I like
I need their words for my poems, to speak for a
house we make together that's fragile and strong
shaky in an American wind contrary to poetry
And I get scared and children's bodies
are often feverish, those whom
you love more than yourself (though not more than
poetry) so what can you do, send them to school and hope

they survive the violence of the human mind bent
on impressing itself into them. Flow of atoms of
sorrow and ecstasy, they were never my own body
I was the case for more people arriving why not.
My saint's T-shirt, she's howling but
not against natural exigency, I'm poet and not much else
I ripped out a normal face
and gave my kids the archaic voice of poetry

Place Myself in New York (Need One More There)

We move to New York so I can be wild language briars
Oh is that why? I try everything to write
My desire's extraction of woman from myself onto paper
To put her there as if she were. And to put him there speaking
Back and forth rosewater and glycerine either/both
Softening and scenting facts of no money and ensuing death.

This isn't plain it wasn't so plain an ill man
For example I'm married to but I sing "Just
A poet" he'd described me the highest compliment
Not a diva experimentalist genius or ferocious outlaw---
Just a poet. Who am I I'm really social
For the first time in my life and for years (that's
Over) there are these craftsmen craftspeople everywhere
To find out from. Oh fellow consider

The look of legs walking on film, in the rhythm of
Traffic signals; the permanence of New York light
Embedded into the texture of jeans and plaster and red
Juice, a painting; someone is shouting up from downstairs
No he's shouting his poem to anyone: I'm
Writing it down for him, "Don't shit me man / Just say it out."

I've said everything to you now I'm happy
Kids come here and have hamburgers sun's sunk
Over rooftops leaving trace of whitened dark-blue in dark-blue
I like how small the apartment it pulls us closer
Piezoelectric crystal they've gone to bed now and don't think
Just pick up words not toys. All my best writing down
Done late at night not like this but like that back
Then, my life's disconnections a culture in unitive me

No divinatory gift—no deaths will ever come--
Just a poet, one; corrupted by the competition
Of Who'll say it.

The Trouble with You Girls

In the chair covered with shawls
I'm wearing my favorite red shirt
Maybe it's November near my birthday, sun
On my shoulder and coffee too in what cup chipped;
So, happy, open a blackbound notebook.
Ted pulls on one of his colored T-shirts,
"The trouble with Jackoff is   no the trouble with *you* is"
(Because I'm not listening) "you're stuck in that chair"
It's true. I sit, wait for the greatest
Poem I'll write   "Just want
To drink things and write rocks off." What else?
I don't know what I'm for To praise, he might say
I don't think so. "You have no philosophy," he says,
"That's the one thing you need to be great."
I'd fight back, but the buzzer rings, Marion
She comes over daily, before everyone else
In her halterneck denim jumpsuit, anemic, what's
A person for Answer me late 70's. I think it's
Partly to be with a plant, that potted begonia
What's *it* for, I try to hold it alone in my mind
Without a thought *of* it, just it, as red and green light.
Marion and I have coffee. Day's lovely before I'm
Too many thoughts, I've become content this year;
In October, without looking down I climbed out
On the fire escape, cleaned my window
I see you through me now, not just me, I think.
"The trouble with you girls   you think it's all
Sunshine and coffee. It's money, lots of it
Everything's money My ass is money, yours too
Even if your asses aren't as ugly as mine   Got any
Money for cigarettes, Marion?" Marion and I
Cleaned this apartment, when I first took it and
It was so small, before everyone came in.
"How about a little extra, for a pepsi, and the paper?
How about some doughnuts for us all?"

Self '78 Speak

It isn't art now all my mistakes are still there
probably because I tried so hard to be in the world.
Can I ever be alone in New York, I don't want to be
What would I find? that I don't need such attention
Oh don't we all want to be adored, and to adore
art heroes? Beneath the forms of adulation
I must know that real love's impersonal   I express
personality a present's shape for you, friend; but when
I learn a new poetry technique, I'm shaken and changed.
This love isn't play anymore and I'm not it personally

Steve there you are with your flaw; all you really like
are lines of poetry—not just your own but
whatever comes directly from nature in genuine light.
I'm thinking how you've just said "distemper" so fondly
I'm walking inside falling snow, at night, in a scarf
Outside away from everyone can think of myself characteristically
as anonymous girl the poet; or as in the machine of
poetry moving closer and closer to its center, which is not
mechanistic something so frightening to Steve and me
that we can't face it.

                    Ted says he
and Tom believe in god and Steve and I don't.
Their bad habits—all three—are much worse than mine
so is that a victory of course not am I different I don't know
'I don't have to tell you everything and I never have.'
I guess I've gone out for the pepsis and beers, who owns
the corner store the Portuguese family, Johnny and Michael's dad
will die of a mysterious illness   we run a small tab there.
The night's full of people who are like us, but not
in their words for what happens: I feel closer to them than
to most poets but I can't live without our words.

1979 A Dream

I'm a saint because first I have such vertigo
standing at the window of a bottomless building
in fear of least motion towards space
Reed and Anne nearby, especially Reed for his name
I'm so pliant and bowed so crushed I
can't find I, I'm, at all—such a dot
an air-bit in this thousand-year moment
I almost step through the window and never
resolve that *I* won't or don't jump, so later
having only doubted myself I'm naturally
one of the white-garbed saints in Leo Genn's charge
Do you remember Leo? was Petronius in *Quo Vadis?*
opened his veins under sentence from Nero
while Xtians were mauled, crucified upside-down
We saints have a score of music
and as we sing some are "translated," that is
disappear, a girl evaporates, into a plane of
some spiritual existence, of which I'm almost
terrified because the lack of self there must be total
Where does she go, what is it like?
it's like loss of everything we give us
it's like what the real given is, the given
is nothing to fall or descend from to
succeed with rebel against condemn or turn evil in—
and so it seems like negation since
it isn't anything we value
and so the notes in the music are deep holes
and when she goes, the translated girl
nothing's left not a flicker no gold:
I dream this dream in the late seventies
How can I desire such
translation, I want the world as we see, hear,

in my score; to hand you the
music of St. Mark's Place on paper
blue-black sirens a suffering I
perceive as rooted in each sufferer's
simultaneous transcendence of it and
those who don't suffer are the doomed, the idiot
Neros

The Year of the Premonitory Dream That Ted and Steve Left Me

Because this room's a community of voices
I have self as urban social graces
Red colors suggesting streaks of flame
Crawl into my hat and I'll talk to you, taking to heaven
Whose fucking heaven? (*She* thinks if
Everyone did what she says, sexually and to her, it
Wouldn't be a Nazi, that world, but I think so)
    Who said the Chesterton stuff
St. Francis of not a sissy—and X thinks
She's a star Y thinks she's a saint, and we call them, in fact,
St. Marsh Gas and St. Carnivore, not very funny
Rising to the level of protecting oneself against their
Henry James component—*did* I say Harry? in this den of,
I'm gonna put you down some more, 'cause I like to.
Another entrant: I've just arrived, I'm a man in a belt, and
I think you're cute. So we talked like this for about six years
With excursions, for example, aside to consider the arrival
Of the Language Poets onto their Gilligan's Island.
Two pinkies a greenie two aspirin and a beer and soon you
Best intensity female, man you have almost made it
George says oil ruined the history of art
Allen comes in and says, this smells of speed that cum on your pants?
No, Elmer's glue of course—look Eileen's leaning
Various faculties upon me. The world has unrestrained me,
Writing deranged in space and time splashed with Pepto-Bismol
So I won't have to seem blue. I never or always
Loved you   remembering all the times I was bad
Including now? Bad bad bad. Gradual loss of vision
This is an impersonation, in exactly another costume,
Of 1979, the year I was social ware most had
Married world. Like a quilted velvet boxing glove

An illuminated stage which melts onto page a *New York Post* Modern
Ted says he's a spaniel puppy, yap, and four more people come up
Two Tibetan nuns who take tea. What is your pretty self doing?
It's only a hatchet job on *your* reality   oh
Just Bohemia I see, as if the fucking middle class and the
Vicious fucking upper class and the whole nightmare
Class of others in their purses weren't a class of affectation too
And the stupid fucking workers voting Republican!
Ask him to write a poem that contains the following phrases
United Nations, Simone Weil, optic nerve and mother-of-pearl—but
He couldn't he's an academic! He just couldn't, his dad's dog
Died on the road in his last poem. Come on
Put it on the paved area adjoining the house:
That's a patio see, if you only said the definitions
Of nouns instead of the nouns you'd sound more interesting.
But they want to sound boring they said so I read it
In his already collected crit This guy
This guy's been dead since before *I* died and he's
Younger, Grace and certain salvation, yeah, ain't for
My ship on fire. Five or six ships are on fire here Peggy
They'll never make it to port, put out the rug flames
Hannah says, I'll pour boiling water on the rat.
Gradual loss of vision, Johnny A lot of activity, lovely
And twisted fingers as from hard work, it *was* hard work, Elinor
We made twenty-five dollars, we leaked everything that we had
We were escarpment, espousal, imbecile, and change.

Hematite Heirloom Lives On
(Maybe December 1980)

I saw him bleeding but I thought all blood was a dream.
Certainly I had none.

I may be making erotic art near the red telephone
that connects Ted to his mother dying of cancer
I cut out photos of nude women and place them on food signs
Chicken Pot Pie. Why—because I want to save
the women in the photos, so make them humor-filled or
truly connected to the fountainhead of sex as I imagine it.
She holds the most amethyst grapes to her breasts
I've cut out her face it's off howling in space
sex is for god because it's a furious
violent brightness so I make a straw fetish
with a red tonguelike clitoris to protect me
from literature and from my dear friends. The women don't
approve the men do I ignore them but this is minor I want
to be there to describe the harmony between the fact
that I make these collages and write "Waltzing Matilda"
that and the red phone to Peg. That and all the speeches
        which must be made
by Ted in the other room waiting for bad news for years.

Oh kids life is feelings like these it's the talk of it
        drawing
the others outside to our house: the news is throughout us
the mondial flames of hell, the funniness, we are
        unironized.

Yet I keep not being able to be there. From now it's because I'm
still hurt. As sweet as pain to a saint is the door
to the actuality of those events.
Will the door open. Not unless I
give up my fear of my anger I'm just a girl from the desert

am I. I'm still so angry at people I know, I can't go in.
How many of you sexist feminists think I'm only part of him
          part of him?

You, I remember you then.
You said goodbye to me, outside on
the streetcorner, two years later, because I was "part of him"
and you were making war with him—-though I
wasn't to take it personally You were too much trouble anyway
you always had to be adored. You made me say
I love you; I lied; I've adored no person.
Love isn't your present, you can't ever have mine I
don't *own* a love; saying goodbye now, then

the pizza shop there (from where I once saw, in subzero
          weather
at night, a naked man barefoot streak by)
the tawdry bar's over there; I want to win this poem, don't I
a poem can't be won by a person, I can't come out of this one
clean I'm too mean; though there's
the cleaners there, and even the sneakers store, four
          corners crossroads

I'm telling the truth. I'm going to tell it
anyone's: that never being what anyone thought
I never cared what anyone thought
as long as I could go home, and resume my work—-am I
back in the door? Oh Ted's here, kids asleep, dark window dreams
oh airshaft dark window I often mistake for
the panelike sails of a clipper ship taking us home.

C. '81

People with more money than us
don't seem to
trust us (not strictly true)
We have hardly any, ever
Maybe they shouldn't trust us
we're always looking to borrow
five ten or twenty dollars
we only want to have
just enough money, today
    they think it all "goes for pills"
how much do they think pills cost
we have no
expensive habits I mean as in
other people's worlds
clothes, travel, decor, enter-
tainment we do buy books we don't have a
phone for seven years, no checking account

Of course I'm not being objective it was my life
As a matter of fact I feel positively defiant about it
I liked our economics they were transparent
I understood money thoroughly
I had guilt from borrowing
but never the guilt of having something
the only thing that suffered was Ted's
health it suffered considerably

I can't get at the poem of this
I think of '81, '82 as rather ugly years
casting cold shadows black
against the sky of a sun disappearing
but back to economics
nobody trusts the poor
the poor are more interesting than others

almost uniformly
they're crazed resentful struggling paranoid excessive
anxious about their faded rickety possessions
and their stoops
their patches of sunlight or shade on stoops
their children going wrong
and all the disorder of the garbage cans
everyone else boringly has
clean cold spaces new things
private schools self-filled conversations
rooms full of shadow where rage should be
and the voices
of people subject to the fits of
demonic radios in their heads
well I've had my radio implant at times
and known people with louder ones
everything the voices scream about
relates to money one
way or another

I'm being self-righteous so
I can own my own past again
and so my present, no bondage or confinement
of shame of not making money
it's a talent people are born with—poetry isn't it's
life's condition poetry's so common hardly anyone
can find it
money's common but much more cornerable
poetry's air and money's ore—a certain mineral
that slides across distances into hands it fits
born with a hand shaped like money they say, that
cute clean white hand

I can't get to the poem of this
though I choke with it again being there
in another decade being here's not much different
the rage of unremunerated work—

can't you hear the voice in my head
can't you hear this fucking voice in my head
of course I'm not right I'm never right
I'm fucking lazy unskilled and you deserve your money

Gladly Though I Lost It and Knew I Would

This is a community of a handful
four frail humans in a third story apartment
nest of boards slapped together with glass
Aren't we all fragile, two of us children
I don't get how we have imagined
our world and it's imagined us
I'm yellow T-shirt jeans messy haircut
Who told one to have what life from
categories with numbers of stars viz
one star housewife two stars office maybe
three stars professional four
stars and above why that's famous and
what stars am I? abuser no stars?
But anyone's an abuser—in my
girlish depths I'm untouched by
drug or drink but not complicity
in the abuse of the whole substance of a city
or crime of possession that encompasses
the country, don't we possess, abuse it
together, this country from which we abuse
the substance of the world?
So we—not you—live in a treehouse
I have them to love, can't see far beyond
but I say, Help me write, to the words
and the words say, Here are the words
because the words love me and not you
I found them where there was much less abuse
in this dark and electric light-sea
no-water sea of much salt blown in freely
for sagacity and pain-in-wound and drying up
light's drying up he's almost overstayed his
term of abuse
                        And do I misuse my time saying
Give me some more words please
You know you can't run

the world from here he says
you don't write like
the fuckers like—and
isn't that good in the longer run
of mysterious currental change
flowing from the future alive now, you?

In our apartment we have imagined
a world which abuses much less
and imagined his encroaching death
or did we forget to imagine that, did we
imagine our affection only, "our best work"?

We were tenderness, as small community
and more that than any way we fucked up
god knows there's so little "So little
tenderness in American poetry" as
Robert Duncan once told me—who was he?
Who was anyone? unstarred brightest equality

We rejected power in the third-story nest
and so we had tenderness
but no sense or money you might say
sense that's what they say and so

      tenderness
      doesn't fail
      real life needs only
      so much power takes
      only a bit
      to make a presence
      a word or two
      on paper
      like

    "gladly, though I lost it, and knew I would"

How We Spent the Last Year of His Life

Ted's mother Peggy dies in July and Ted dies the following July
the year between a painful mess; it's raining as usual in Paris
who would want to talk of this and if I don't the book's diminished
in its exploration of a self, I'm speaking of a dying person
embedded in certain ways self to self with me: how will we
extricate each other, to exist as separate essences?
How do we spend the last year of his life though, bitterly
fighting with friends   This poem is prosaic. "Danger waters
coming" remember that song, he refers to it in a poem
the day before Peg dies, or is it that day, "Hold me tight."
I haven't the heart——oh prosaic still——not, to hold you tight
but to tell the whole silly story, the deeply traumatizing trivial
events of the entirely censored censorship, of a remarkably short
collaborative poem of ours, from a downtown mimeo magazine,
presumably because it contained the word "motherfuckers"?
Question-mark stet; because I'm still pissed off. We tried
to draw attention to this outrage, but were rebuffed as druggies
from Hell by our locals including the anti-censorship champions
of the world. I'm obviously not saying the names, that's not the
       poetry The poetry's
when you lie asleep beside him and dream of his Egyptian tomb;
when for months while he's asleep you wake up and look to see if he's
breathing, though you're only admitting to yourself, "He
may just have a few years more." No that sounds like prose.
We didn't feel welcome at the Poetry Project anymore. He writes
       a lovely
poem about us as and watching Fred Astaire and Joan Leslie in
a less wellknown movie. Can all this be to the point?
A self's good a fragile house that doesn't fall. (And the bad are
good too   I don't know what I mean; I seem to be a crypto-Christian——)
The magic in death, it opens the ground, and when the dying one
disappears, like Oedipus at Colonus, the alive one's both
devastated and exalted. Because the poetry's beneath the prose

of whose bad behavior ours or theirs. One is fatigued with behavior
in 1983 and now; and the behavior of some others, for me, will stay
        trapped in
the place of death's mystery That's a mystery too, that blemish
        on purity, and
how hard it is to forgive. Not rationally· that's easy; but truly
A soul your self can't get free of your actions, watch your step
        (prose not poetry).

The Common Ground Ask Anyone You Know

"knows you better than
you know yourself"

lazy unimpaired and unoriginated
there if I ask if it's there
because what I do at best is respond from
it in kind
after all
I know how to hear *you*

it is my automatic goodness
when it's blocked I'm shamed
it conflicts with self but is true self
as
I'm grouchy
when Ted is dying
because performing my magic function
of complying exactly with his needs is not
in harmony
with our life's everyday surface I am
gargoyle so he can be
grace—
well there are two cases here two deaths
and in one
I plead crudely
that Daddy die (the doctor prompts me)
removal of feeding tubes and such
in the other I *am* a grouch
nearby but somewhat ill-tempered
and then I rise to the occasion its
unexpected
shock but first feeling only a
reluctance to

get up from my chair
and then after brief words
he's gone forever

of course I've lost track of where I was
in this "argument"
I was dark substance in
those situations
oh it flooded me in New York
after the second of those deaths
bits of gauze and equipment still on
the scarred wooden floor (with Murphy's soap
I tried to soften that floor later
make it look ancient not tenement-like)

as it flooded me then, does still
this Knower this
knowing of me
which is a ground of
affectionate
action—I know I

don't think with myself
do with
myself or with people only
there is this blackness inside unmechanical
a sort of
breath
that isn't always
breathed

Point of Fidelity

Taking a large bloody napkin upstairs
Then eat a blue heart-shaped valium
with a red dot on it

Why can't I live as I say
barren wilderness beauty I say?

offer a right poverty
sitting near my sandals
throw away these feelings I'm so
        easily tricked by
poems of smallness I'm so easily, others'
        easy reception of a heart-mind
a simulacrum

Took the bloody napkin upstairs
then took a blue heart tranq

What's the name of the larger island?
Why am I still on the smaller one?
I'm not a story or life: if I
say that, I'm suddenly here
terror in this real poem

Bring the bloody napkin upstairs
Don't take the blue heart tranq

A great thing is of no importance
Hooked, and tricked, like a criminal
on greatness, a flourish a sound of a fiction

What is the true name
it's I not 'so she' 'so she'
Face the air and say I
Go past tears don't be 'moved'

There's catastrophe, a poem
"I keep seeing all those bodies"
Wrench back from a fiction
The bodies are really there then
Catastrophe is in the real poem

Took the blue kotex upstairs
Took the bloody tranq

swallowed the heart
so I wouldn't have to be
"I keep seeing all those bodies"
Who am I responsible to?
A self, precisely, and "all those bodies"

Don't dance on the bodies
"What does she think she's doing
asking me to dance with her on his grave?"
I remember saying that once:
to accuse of the wish to dance
is almost to dance, to dance on the
mechanistic wrongdoer

mechanistic oneself, as if a character
in some stupid novel, perpetually, daily
reserving my real self
for a confrontation in the future

And so face it now face it
what I am, infinite and
"all those bodies"

Flashback to
a consecrated time a proper
instance in a wilderness:

POEM

This death is Egyptian
I wear an Egyptian dress
with black horizontal stripes
you even say "your dress is Egyptian"
when I perform your last rites
sprinkling you with drops of gin & tonic
and saying, "May the 14 pieces
of Osiris be joined together"
We laugh though you'll die the next day
Eleven years later I wonder
at using such a fiction, a fetish of Egyptian
exactly to be there, that moment.

Things we do together can be
          true, actions true
"I keep seeing all those bodies"
Take the bloody napkin upstairs
Open the pupil, tranq-less in terror
hollowware hollowware
filled with self
                    Living is a poem,
ask an animal
What else is it doing there, sifting genes?
I take the bloody kotex upstairs
I don't have to put it in my trash
your trash will do too.

I—Towards a Definition

Grief isn't empty it's black and material I've seen it
It's a force, independent, and eats you while you're sleeping
The spring after Ted died I once saw it in pieces
in the air of the apartment tatters
whirled around me like burnt paper

I know I didn't make it what made it
Could hardly stand up some days that year because of it
No luxuriance in this process no dolorous
sea of grief it's a battle
Pieces of myself are hacked away my adulthood is
art a lost story

What's left of me really is a young girl
and to accept her after such war, after the tears of
myself as a general have hardened into semiprecious
ivory or coral, is sad and
defeating no victory
Oh yes this is who I always am
beginning child literal I
I'm myself so, knowing a new thing, that
the universe is ruled by love and countervalent sorrow
Grief's not a social invention
Grief is visible, substantial, I've literally seen it

II—The Person That You Were Will Be Replaced

In grief the person that you were is replaced by grief
not the person you originally were but the one you'd become.

Grief is opportunistic and uncontrollable
    it doesn't exactly come
from you, you "allow it in"   It's godlike
    as in possession.

This was the night I was the craziest: near my birthday,
four months after Ted's death, walking
on Second Avenue I thought "It's possible
he didn't really die." I felt a maniacal joy
and then became sickened and distressed
I knew a depth of me had, up to then, believed he was alive.
That depth was now emptied of him and filled with grief.

I dreamed all that year; I divided into dreamer and interpreter
    A gigantic horse blocks
    the entrance to
my building; I wake up and think "The horse is a hearse"
    blocking my life. Or
a dream with a dawn in it, the sky purple-black,
but a hint of dawn, and when I awake I know it's the sky
in Lawrence's "Ship of Death"—thin white
thread—trying its way

                    If a self can
contain the deaths of others, it's very large;
it's certainly larger than my body
    If the other who dies is partly me,
and that me dies and another grows, the medium it grows in
    is grief.

———

The wish to locate absence, that contemporary obsession to
      find the empty present—
grief will saturate the present.

Grief isn't glandular; though becomes somatic;
gets far into your body Eats it changes it.

One is magically struck down at certain
moments, can't move, can't arise,
and inside is poison: grief gets caught
in intensifying pockets which when opened
cause sensations of illness. On Christmas morning
I can't stand up.

If you immerse your feet in icy water
you forget grief for a moment. I did this once, my
brother-in-law made us cross a cold stream barefoot,
that winter, walking in the woods—I was emptied, then elated,
blissful; but didn't try it again. Grief
returns vengeful after you've repulsed it.

Flowers

I was there because of the poetry
I thought it only grew in really dirty dirt
And there was so much of it everywhere
Ugly-beautiful red rag petals, folksongs of agitation elation
Waving streaming or floating in or through bad air

I lived in a lovely redpetal slowly burning house
On fire because
I lived in a situation which would end
With someone who would die because
Ill-health, excess, poverty, neglect
Are a common sight along roadsides
Orange to scarlet then deep blue as I always say

And so some of it we did and some was done to us
Of the so-called negative characteristics and happenstance
Some of the flowers were ugly and leathery
Swamp-stink brown-spotted fights
I'm not being clear, we had inappropriate emotions
The American poetry vacant lot's small and overgrown

So you squabble with everyone
That can be healthy or vicious
When someone's dying for years
He does and doesn't say so: We sip at our sweet poisons
Jewel-colored legendary chemicals
At our emotions splenetic and ecstatic
We are used for various purposes in return for subsistence
But it's always hoped that one
Will contain oneself
Will you not overflow into the lot
As anything beyond your dirt as
Prophecy cry-for-help cry-of-rage cry-of-too-much
Love cry-of-knowledge, not overflow?

I feel that the others don't want to know
Speaking even now as a later presence.
But in order to be honest
I must change my poem
Drastically, can't get there this way—
I am now the poet in this story

I have a headache in a burning house for years
Hardly know that it's burning
Then after the death-event itself
There's threat of flood and drowning
Scatter marijuana on the waters
To quieten them—is Atlantis sinking?
Nothing so grand as that dream in our lot
Where I'm still choked in dense clusters
I must leave the lot of flowers
To find a purple female cunt-lipped tree
"Drink of the spring inside me"
Water in a tree
This water's really dark and purple
Deathlike and dangerous and free
And drink of it if you can; she says, "I'm
The laurel tree"
But if I drink of her who knows it
If I've drunk from the actual tree
Who can tell except her and me?
Laurel's not for the public head it's a
Secret intoxication
I wonder if this is an obnoxious poem
I wonder if it's really understood that
Poetry and I are its subject, not
The death of a husband in neglect
It's my neglect I'm entranced by
And my garland of the everlasting laurel leaves
Evergreen darkgreen elliptical thick and bunched

A Metaphysics of Emotion

The cosmos or void a cloud with a gold crust under it.
This is a vision, that it—what I will be after my life—
is a plain of expanding cloud with a gritty gold underside
I feel the gold crust inside myself as a melting
      the give of dying ice.

Sex begins again in widowhood accompanied by
other visions—that there's liquid gold script on the inside of
my abdomen; that I'm enclosed in midnight-blue
      it's the color of
Isolde's and Tristan's forest—which is only my own
      park Tompkins Square
expanding from a hidden thicket into woods in which
I'd gladly stay with you, die and decay to a handful of bones.

One by one snowflakes gathering at night in the purple-gold
      light of the lamp
out my window on St. Mark's Place. I'm turning into colors—
      red, dark-blue, gold, black—
together an emotional field that is more than emotion the
      word might suggest:
it's emotion as atoms, as matter of our being and of the
      being before this world.

Sex destroys creation until there's issue and therefore
      is dangerous.
The lovers in the forest for two years, eating colors
      a metaphysical existence
texture counter to our world which is calling me to be
      created
in the image of irony, judgment, and jokes—the kind that
      establish superiority
or territory, piss on the sidewalk. *My poetry is too heavy*
      now, isn't it.

I'm creating myself enlarging from a fleck of gold or blue
        sapphire
a snowflake next to a notion of a ruby the two falling
        together
on a collage I make   flowing into the center of a disallowed
        metaphysics:
language didn't kill him   grief isn't a word   I'm not a
        person

Becoming Egyptian

I see myself becoming a more generalized
person after Ted's death
try to change those lines, make them more
vivid, but they're blowing away
gold chains in dark air at night then— ·

Besides what I still won't tell.

I'm beginning to want to write an epic poem.
or a very thick poem   since time's thick for me
poem could be long vertically, not linearly
as I now am, but this description's as dull, as I often was—
"long" "thick" "dull," a walking repository, of my ancient history
but my names and my dates are of no interest to me poetically
and more than history I'm geology; though am not I
except so purely there's nothing to say of it a grave a canyon.

I want to go as far back in time as
will comfort by causing my life not to have been.
But can never get far enough. all's the image of modernity cast
        backwards
And the women slaves. Even Queen T'iy's broken face. in the Met
        she's just a closed mouth
she's not beautiful, the fragment is beautiful *she's*
not, this piece of a statue is   she isn't a queen she's a piece of
        fucking rock
the Egyptians are stupidly, specifically, sociological like I
        seem, in my
hopeful new clothes, my skirt with buttons, my shoulder pads.

I have a lover —that story's still mine,
for you a jewel in design the light hovering, angelic or
        unethical.
but focus on me alone, so I can think.
This book will change. It has to. I know I'm finally of no

importance, as the promulgator of my details, because I've
been so violated. Yet I'm not the promulgator of my society's
details, as the thought of the 80's would have it

I am now the mystery of this book.
Thus will cease to speak so much of myself.
As details, pieces. Can't find myself in them there.
As a one a life. A self is bigger than that because death has
entered it, and reenters it
making a largeness of it, empty of plot;
contains other people's seeming plots, or, wistfully, the sketch
     of a plot
it can't stay interested in. I leave lines in space but
I forget them.

Mid-80's

I'm not on a mission
I'm not local
I have never been so, though I'm
local to my condition of being a widow
Obviously I'm more serious than these times

Keep on being my times
Why am I wearing these women's clothes
Earrings with magic stones
to ward off the weight of my feelings
to adorn the vacancy of the times

I am a secret when everyone else seems
some sort of pastel whore
selling it blandly for not having sex
pussy and prick for no sex
offered up without a smell to an age of making it

I'm not my life now or yours
blackberries wears a blackberry dress
because I'm a widow wear a black lace mask
Is there a present? never
The 80's is the weakest, the least existent ever

Strike a spark off a pinhead
Trying to get lost in it being bigger than it
the so-called present one sings an
adulterous song   This music is pure, pure
But secret

The poor say that in their desperation
they invent a sensuous music
Those with money can take it away
Can take music and sex away?
By making it records and porn: suppress our insides

——————

There's no self in the 80's don't you know
Say there is none and be selfish
Empty the glass of sexuality   Fill it with
Madonna's piss
analyze it thoroughly write a book

I behave badly, to capture sex
My love is to conceal myself
How much am I my life?
It feels as if others have stolen
my life, my old music, my culture—

even my alcohol's been stolen
In place of a life they have images
When a whole country a world becomes
moronic, that must be willful
It isn't that easy to be stupid, is it,

why *am* I wearing these clothes?
waiting to be colors, love, that glow
from the shock of physical contact
radical contact, a scarlet cloth torn
beneath a glass dome where it snows

Inside a time are its lies
There seems nothing else in the 80's
No one did anything but lie for years
Not just the pols, the artists the poets
concealing their bodies and voices—

there's hardly a prosody now
I was dead I was stupid that way
didn't see the advance of such organisms
They took over by denying everything as rich as
fucking or grieving or singing

Why don't I have a kinder voice

to send into the helpless past?
Because it's not helpless, it's still going wrong
the love there's concealed not concealing
Who took our lives and gave them

to industry of every kind of image
make and wear them, see and listen
teach and learn them—they're us
pieces of appropriated authority
legitimize my crumb so I can sell

I've always wanted the whole love that is,
a poetry not in pieces:
love conceal nothing, and hate?
Though I loved in it I hate that age
I don't want to engage in more politesse with it

I'm not on a mission, I'm not local
Poetry's global, everyone
participates in the same poem
Into it we project our demons
ourselves torn out of us in dangerous clothes—

make an age like the 80's worldwide
I'm still watching, in '94
the men of careers proliferate, though
in the 80's I'm in shadow
fascinated by the shadow's silkiness

by the secrecy of my mutation
I feel as if I'm becoming something I
already should have been
eroticized, spiritualized
by tragedy, surviving in darkness

Most people's currency is such survival
Tragedy's the name of some dirt

it's rich, it purges and redeems
but some people never change and they're always
in charge of suppressions and lies

You Can Give It Away

In the last four years little gustatory pleasure
I'm at JFK airport drinking a white wine cooler
Trying to write in a notebook ungamely white
Iterated motel-like walls
                        With a relief on them of a red girl sailing
I'm waiting for a plane to Luxembourg May '87
To be a poet for a week in Europe
                        In my natural history
I can't find the bottom of my glass where I see through
Clearly to more than a pluvial dampness
Of my original self
                Who was ever here?
That modern reddish girl on the wall's ill-starred to be remains
Of a fashioning impulse:
                        Bad art
Am I bad art?
                I'm going away to find you
I haven't written well for a while, which do I want more
Poetry or life? I will want you quickly, not so much as if
I saw through a glass to only you
                                But as if we were both
The walls of my glass without you I'm no structure
                                        To hold the form
Of scrutiny itself I've no eyes' sides

                                Go to Luxembourg Hurry
It's foreign and take a nap
                        Go to festival party
Poets arriving, "Here come the English," says someone, "they
        go off and drink a lot"
There you are
                With Wendy, Allen, Ken, all serious-faced out the window
You buy me a langouste later—How long will this take? three
                                        more nights
Till we leave for Paris together

———

But in Luxembourg still myself I buy socks
Eat at McDonald's alone, amused

                          In predestined Paris
You have a Blue Lagoon

                      I have a Kir Royale, then Duck
There's something I have to tell you

                             In two more days that I've given you myself
I mean if I think of going back alone it—myself—isn't there anymore
I panic slightly walk out get lost

                         Between your place
And the Grands Magazins

                I've already given it to you
So if I can't give it to you

                It's lost somewhere, and I am mechanics
Who's speaking

            Who's watching inside me?
(I will get myself back
By giving me away)

But in This World Together and Not Passing Away

"But in *this* world
                together & not
passing away
              things are
together
           seven turquoise sequins and a
golden facial surface, her
        eyes
are violet emptied flowers and a
        crystal, and a
mouth, her eyes are
        a mouth
her spokes are golden lamé of spokes
        Her atlas
is high above among the
        birds   "

In those years, when I wrote that poem, the heat was off a lot.
This description of a fan I'd made a collage of paper and objects upon
an ordinary spoked paper fan   this fan
was particularly cool with surfaces of foil and sequin and crystal
cold-looking and -touching in heatlessness a fan likely made in
        January
it contains a drawing by me of a goddess with
flowers and crystal for senses, against a backdrop of suggested
        height and rare aether

Kate of course dies in summer the fan is more blazing then
Sandy asks for an object perhaps a fan she says
to accompany Kate on her journey by cremation to
the other air, so I select that fan —I've already written the
        poem of it—
with its light weight of gold crust—-paper—the crystal is
        its only burden

A work of art to
be burnt up for love but
art doesn't last long anyway
a civilization's an instant that
Kate lived as long as, in cold cosmic terms
in dreams still she says she loves me but she's Sandy's;
of course; my problem's not with that but
with loss of brightness, eclipse of the golden
(a Renaissance poet's theme) She is the sun blotted out,
"She was my little girl," I say, crying the day after
I don't mean she's like my daughter, I mean that she'd been
the little girl and then an older radiant friend, but girl, my lost
      girl spirit

her eyes are violet emptied flowers her heart is a crystal
her senses the seven (including affection and rationality)
turquoise sequins, floating above the Atlas Mountains
when my life's over it will be just as over as hers, or a
      locust's, so
time is destroyed then so is destroyed now, it wasn't
time, her life   neither hot nor cold, it was her crystal

The New York Human

The summer bum is back, Nick suggests to Diane
she might like to sleep with the S.B. on
his new mattress that someone threw out
she just giggles flattered to be thought sexual
no I was never guilelessly dispossessed
that means homeless I guess
I don't know what anyone's like
anymore understand less and less
of the nature of the hustle for status
if you live in the present you're alive in others'
gaze calculated cruelly sized up

Whose gaze can I stand
I'm writing for unseen strangers   no I'm
cave in head writing to be sense of
self, man in blanket on sidewalk
I know he's just like me though if he
says something about my cunt
I won't like him what a stupid animal he'll be
someone else looks up and says "He don't mean nothing"
money is morals, better people always
have more of it clean housed and carred
everyone holds onto theirs oh so assiduously
we have an art collection
for which we've never paid anything
sell off bits for the overdue bills
a small Warhol to a millionaire for a few hun
(Rene has fits) our art is our morality
like everything we seem to give it away

Over the years the poets and artists
become more moral   skirted women
"All I want is proper publication" I say that
Then why don't you write a double sestina?
form is money yes form is morality

I tell Sparrow I hate the art of that man
who puts broken crockery and knickknacks
in plaster around all the lampposts
who ever heard of a street in New York
becoming like a section of a folk art park
behind the College of Chiropractic in Davenport Iowa
the last supper rendered all in seashells
fuck that guy and his shoe and his dog Blue too

Doug and I are becoming slightly more moral
"What shall I say in my double sestina?" I ask him
he replies, "Any broken phrase in plaster
will do in these postmodern times, you asshole"

I Am a Hardened Heart

Sisters and mother who look like me
Then, who is my self?

Dream of us in white sequins
in the house of a dying aunt
but it might be my old bedroom on Waveland—
crystals in a geode, frozen
in meld in the center of a rock.

I gave you a black dress and a vintage
forties red dress: John Ashbery
had told me he wished he could wear it.

I gave you a jasper brooch an oval landscape mountain-and-
        cloud-like
reminds me of my unpublished poem, "Inside the Smoky Quartz
Crystal"—in which the rock and I talk—too much of a
conjunction for *Conjunctions*.

You gave me driftwood, and you gave me lapis
and you gave me malachite, turquoise, and crystal
I gave you amethyst, jet, and amber
I gave Al amber and I gave Daddy seashells
and also mixed stones—I was given citrines
(and Kate gave me her citrines) and I was given topazes, jade,
and pink and black coral.

I call you up and my voice startles you, you say "You sound
        like me."

Can't talk about you the same way as the dead
or myself—or other poets, or,
airily, American nation
Are or aren't similar kinds of stones—but stones
are similar, binding the earth and souled in

the universal way—our universe is more
rock and air, more geologic process than human
or animal or vegetal—it's planets of rock and weather—
to us, dead soil.

Is that most of what is, what is it doing
what is "doing"?
I give you stone, you give me stone

first geodes in '64, we share one of amethyst
you give my sons rock collections
trilobite, cinnabar, smithsonite

a matrix is a womb I thought it was a rock bed
we've named a whole universe after humans
it probably names us after rocks
not after mothers or
the short time before we harden.

Al gave us sex rocks:
"just another fucking rock"
and amethysts agates and Apache tears
You gave her garnets and you gave me sardonyx
and gave her a pearl and her, opals
I gave myself a Madeira topaz and yellow jade and red crystal
you gave me rosy quartz, amber, and black glass.

The Brain Is a Toy but Loyalty's Metaphysical

He's behind those bushes playing, I don't have to think of him
a brother where it's burnt (he knows about pictographs there
for years), but it's black and brown and beige there hot
shadeless behind the short bushes and down the ravine

I can't catch his nature—who wants a brother?
Momma he won't stop etcetera

I need to show you me and my brother young in the desert
there's nothing to show I'm back there
he's a too younger boy a drag and there's nothing special
None of it's my destiny, how can a brat be
my destiny? in the way that a male politics engulfs
an infinite personal sphere of oneself
and tinges it with tragedy that sickly human invention
not sorrow but tragedy a man-choice made eons ago?
He the little brother is sitting legs splayed out from knees
or he's running in shorts the rocky gully his element

I saw it last week doesn't change much
Maybe they won't fill it in now
because the pictographs are registered
finally

       now those others those
more famous pictographs
the giant man and the giant woman,
several miles outside of town, can
only be seen from the air,
seen properly, and you know then
it's a man it's a woman, so
my obvious point is
our outlines mine and his can perhaps
only be seen from a distance miles up
but that's if you want to see a man and a woman—

I don't really want to
I want to love my brother
loyalty cuts through and is the depths of my nature
I has no quote marks around it (without
distance) I comprehend him

Sept 17 / Aug 29, '88

We get out of the car and I think
I see him, he waves, coming from a woods.
Looks like our dad, shape of head and current
slenderness, mustache; is wearing dark glasses.
Hugs. There's only going to be gladness
at seeing each other We go into
lobby of rehab, Margaret and I get
visitors' tags, girl asks if we're twins.
Al has to give up our birthday presents for him.
He says he can't stand to be inside; we climb a hill
and sit down on a bench. Occasional
interchanges with other patients who
walk or jog past. Mostly we talk about
Vietnam, some about our family
In the afternoon (we've left and come back
with Fred) we sit in a meadow, same
subject matter, some of the same stories. I'll
fuse them. In the morning he was
shaky but not in the afternoon.

"I come back up here all the time. They know where
to find me. (Even if I'm not supposed
to be here, so it's okay.) It's just like Nam
but we'd hear crickets all night there, I hated them.
The nights were terrible. Every night.
I never wanted it to be night just day "
The tank story He's in Quang Tri. Usually
he's the gunner but today for an unremembered reason
the driver There's something called "white
phosphorus" which he's so scared of that
he always fires it off first to get rid of it.
Today's gunner doesn't. What happens is
a shell drops into the small top opening
of the compartment where the gunners are.
Albert hears their screams and knows

everyone is frying from white phosphorus;
he goes for the escape hatch on the bottom, but
it won't open, for long long seconds.
Finally he gets out, everyone else is dead of
course. This is the subject of his most long-
standing nightmare, and first point of guilt,
this escape. "I thought I'd be safe in a tank,
but after that I didn't want to get in one again."
We ask him how he became a sniper "They
came around asking for volunteers. They said
you're a volunteer and *you're* a volunteer,
I was a good shot, good with guns, they thought
I was good. I wanted to be outside. So they sent us
down to sniper school." The snipers would go in
ahead, take a village, then others would follow
Snipers had to kill civilians and "it started
to seem like murder I must have killed 49
or 50 civilians. You see a mamasan with a baby,
you shoot first and ask questions later, she
might be carrying explosives. But they wouldn't
count the civilians in their body count.
They only wanted the NVA. They'd ask if
you got any but wouldn't write it down."
Al witnessed executions by the Phoenix Program.
"They'd come in after we took a village. They had
a list of people to kill. They'd pull up their
hair and shoot them in the head. They'd put down
say, the mayor of a village that was sympathetic to
the Communists, but you could also bribe them
to kill someone in your business you disliked."
The Phoenix Program was CIA-affiliated. (Later
in Needles Dicky Roten confirms that Albert was
in the LRR and a lot of what he did was top secret:
he has a double record, one with blanks.)
Al thinks that at a certain point he was supposed
to die because he knew too much, about the killing of
civilians, Operation Phoenix, and so on.
Members of his sniper unit stopped ever coming back

---

from missions—everything everyone was sent on
was incredibly dangerous. "Then we went into Laos.
The fighting *never* stopped. The Vietnamese Army
was supposed to show up, but they never did.
I got left back with 150 men. If you were left back
it was pretty much assumed you would die. Finally,
everyone was dead except for me and this other guy
We decided there wasn't any sense in staying
since everyone else was dead. We went back to Quang Tri."
It took about seven days. Around 30 miles walking involved.
They caught fish and ate them raw He didn't
know the guy he was with and never saw him again.
"When I got back they were getting ready to send out
an MIA to Mom and Dad. They sent me *instantly*
into North Vietnam. Then I *knew* they wanted to
be rid of me." I think this is when
Albert Trujillo was killed. Albert Trujillo was
Albert's best friend in Vietnam, he was from New Mexico.
He and Albert had sworn to keep each other alive.
N.B. Our dad, also named Albert Notley, had had
a best friend named Albert Trujillo, in Prescott, when
he was Albert's age. But Al's friend Albert was killed
because their sergeant was too slow and scared to cover him.
He let it happen out of fear Albert held a gun then
to the sergeant's head and told him, if you say one word.
Albert brought the body bag back. The last thing
he remembers from North Vietnam is shooting in a circle
all around himself. He got picked up by a chopper,
went back to Quang Tri but it had fallen. Makes his way
down to the South and is eventually shipped home.

I love my brother so much this visiting day, but wonder
if he doesn't know too much to live. He's been
remembering and remembering—the therapists want him
to remember even more, but he doesn't want to, he wants
to go home and see his kids. I wonder how he can
have a future. I want to be able to sit around some
kitchen table with him but can't picture that.

I wonder if he could be the way he was—happier and
lighter—before he started remembering, but
I don't think so. He emanates too much knowledge, power;
his self is huge, bigger than any I've ever witnessed.
His boundaries are too painful and too small:
they keep him where he remembers, they keep his
knowledge concentrated, personal. He must get free of
this self now, but I don't know how he will;
yet escape's fated, written already (we all know it and
don't know it).

Owls

The first owl dream comes a day or two before he dies
there's a bathtub we sit on the edge of— my brother and
I and in the empty tub a reddish owl.
Outside the window, another, a huge gray owl rises up
masses of feathers and intricacy, yellow eyes; behind him
a cartoon woman falls from a ledge.

My father's the great gray isn't he
my brother's the bloody one smaller
and in this dream perhaps Al/owl could not
get purified, in the empty tub so
Al/owl Sr rises through the window as kingdom of
death the great purifier
In a dream some months after my brother's death a tiny
snowy owl pure, sits on the dashboard of my bus
in the snow And then in the dream I've waited for for months
in order to write a long poem——need a dream's inspiration —
in this dream there's a forest and campground, a tent
I approach them as a small owl flies to greet me
reddish and happy, my brother's excited, "He's here!" he cries.
From the tent, with aplomb, a large fierce gray owl walks
My father   wears his liver   outside his body
identifies   himself thus   by his death,   cirrhosis
As you see, I've   fallen into   a measure   like my
poem's   He advises me   on the nature of
this poem as yet   unplanned: it must not   hurt anyone.

I force myself to slip back out of that measure,
the measure of my poem *The Descent of Alette*
in which Alette, the I of it, comes to have characteristics
of an owl. At the poem's end she still has that in
potential, that owl nature——
night, death, war, solitude, wisdom of course but
carnivorousness, silent flight, and camouflage,
protection of her broody funny young.

It's not that we have an 'animal nature'
it's that there's nothing higher or
other, god would be this, it pierces us right through our
houses. Through the flickering thinking I'm
looking, not for my real I but for my real owl.

Vertical Axis

I'm proceeding deeper into the cave
that's enlarging as darkness into sky and earth
a landscape in which there's a cleft a
staircase and deeper, climb down by ladder
rope ladder rungs into a city
the ancient city of   it's lighter brown
ten nine eight steps down to the ledge
what city have I found and below it
excavations in the clay ground
a pit surrounded by the deserted town
and down into the further ground:
A spirit is trapped with black corrugated wings
with pitch dirt soot black wings and topaz eyes
it's I and so I unsophisticated
rises up through the excavation past the
torn ground and some men there familiar
a woman with dyed flame hair
and others holding tablets that will crumble
wings enlarge persuading darkness to support them,
rushing up to change dailiness into the blessing
of unburied joy and a bitterness that must
dissipate into the almond-pale poisonous
morning of a city both smug and desperate
Everyone clinks and walks money of drab imagination
chartering, as that poet said, life into sadness of names, hours,
tenements, supervisors, tiers of power and intellect
description of a tyrant's forehead as the fields of
our painful banality
Over which I-essence flies with its own vengeance
to destroy this city by being realer than
the outlines of buildings and avenues
Don't discount this spirit because it sounds like
what you've named before, poets of texts and charts

and of the civilization you feed and own as you call for change
you would never change, you've smothered change interred it
but I won't be buried in the earth you abuse and slight as
a discarded symbol—nor is I a discarded symbol
I am Alette who, from deeper than the story, can change it.

The Tyrant

I saw you billboard
where are we then?
it won't hurt
a trail of blood, a slice of apple

excavated city walk down
stairs of the excavated amphi-
theater walk walk walk
and on the throne in a pointed crown
the tyranty wise man with wide
grin and blue blue eyes

Make a poem for people to understand
oh why they don't want to understand
except what they already do
middleclass pulings about airless
situations

back to the king, their king
he's also the king of the avant-garde
the king of multicultural poetry
he's the king of communication
king of the form of actualization
everyone makes him king

this isn't nice of you I'm never
          nice now
can't figure out how to be that if
          I must
kill this man over and over in
          order to
exist

He's breaking my heart a jagged red polyhedron

Now that my geometric heart's broken
now that my abstract heart's broken
I gather the pieces, I am the feminist
should I glue them or scatter them everywhere
do I care what I do, except kill him
how did a snake get its culture
by directing its form in the heavenly dust
toward the green brush underneath which
a sign read Do something arbitrary and make it stick.
Then the snake becomes a monarch's stick.
So let's say I say I kill him

kaboom. His hat has fallen
and all the hats in the kingdom too
Do the words on this page, are they owned by him
do the words then slide off and collapse
do I keep on walking do I
do I talk   and what do I say
is it something I already know, from where

Quiet, in this moment again
before starting again   Having
killed him again.

Alette

Long corridor stilled subway
    with polished floors and
black walls

"I now walk into" "this corridor" "lined with cases" "full of the specimens"
"of—it must be—" "civilization," "all guarded by" "a stuffed owl"
"frozen above" "the door" "like a toy a plush" "child's toy"
"Everywhere along" "I survey the" "pained jagged pieces of"

"a worshiped world" "it's my worshiped world" "my turquoise idols"
"carved visages" "of great poets" "coral statuettes" "of couplings, between"
"myself and others" "jade landscapes, onyx" "cityscapes with a white-
    shell moon above" "graven words in gold" "of my own poems, past poems"

"And in a cage stuffed" "my brother stares" "Ted and Kate stare"
"sitting side by side" "and my father" "and some others" "slightly
    shadowed, off to the side" "These are my specimens" "my collection"
"of love and experience   " "In the last case" "my own form

    stuffed and staring:" "in my black coat" "in my long coat" "in which I
    walked down" "into the subway" "and wrote *Alette*" "to break free of such
    frozenness" "It—the writing of *Alette*—" "was alive once" "scalding
    gold of it" "bitter jet black thunderous train roar" "and the quiet caves"

"and quieter still, the" "incomplete dark Paradise" "I hated"
"finishing *Alette*" "and I hate for it" "to be dead in me   " "I have no
    interest, at this moment" "in" "its literary worth"
"All I care about" "is living it" "I want it" "alive again"

"if the owl would live" "I could kill" "another tyrant"
"This hall, this hall is tyrants" "everything in me" "that stays frozen"
"is the tyrant which" "I've made of it" "Where is my real self"
"in this exhibit?" "So I walk on" "down the corridor" "into more"

"darkness where" "there's a lit-up spot" "to stand in" "I step into it"
"and feel feathers grow" "from my skin's pores" "Then the specimens"
"come alive again" "as at a long thin echoing party" "laughing lightly"
"all are graceful" "I can see from here" "how funny Al is" "how radiant Kate"

"And Ted and Daddy have" "one of their conversations" "full of courtesies"
"and secret drinks and jokes" "Now I can fly for I" "was not this world"
"as museum" "I is not a" "museum. my loves live" "and I can leave now"
"I can't relive *Alette*" "can only let it melt" "and my loves live, not

in the past" "but in the present" "I become the owl" "again to leave"
"the underworld" "of my life and" "as a wilder, and more naive and
unimpressionable" "eye I fly away" "the owl flies" "the owl flies"

101

It's possible that I still live there
Apartment that is path-narrow
I don't want to be there in this poem if
Anyone else is, from the past, I want it to be empty
A lot of dust I let fall
It gets smaller   See mobiles from when, a flasher
Whose penis had broken off   That other mobile I
Made it's talismanic objects
A bottlecap a rose a centaur a cactus a coin

Several handmade afghans always and many filthy blankets
Shawls on whatever chair a Mexican shawl a cotton cloth from Africa
What about all of the plants they would get very scrubby
Cunty conches rock collections art everywhere collages and fans
But the apartment's a hallway and odah orange and purple curtains
      at one window
Held up by a rope and hanging clothes tacked up dividing successive
      tiny rooms

Come into the kitchen from outside look down through slanty-floored
      narrow nearly-rooms
The mobiles dangle on the way to the real front room where radiant
      south light is
And there's some light in the kitchen in spring and summer
As well as in the corridorish bedrooms
In the kitchen's a small bathtub underneath it's dark cockroach hell
In the toilet room off the kitchen are the Christmas tree decorations
On top of the kitchen cabinet are dead radios never sent to
      Nicaragua
In the 80's and in the 70's are minor plants on the sill three or four
They look like a few arms reaching malformed something always
      hangs beside the window
A plastic medallion someone once found or a shoehorn
No   the shoehorn was in a bedroom

You had to walk past people in bed to get anywhere
Ted's arm sticks out for some years near the shoehorn where is
    it exactly
And later a photo of Doug's is there of a man looking bored at a
    wrestling match
I've forgotten the books I sold so many for a living more flew back
    the usual and all of Leibling
Fenellosa on art Fat City the Quiller Memorandum was always there
Shibumi the Time/Life Wildlife Series Lévis -Strauss and -Bruhl
All of Stevenson herbals the Mahabharata the First Folio the new
    Tale of Genji the new Proust in the 70's when those were new

There isn't any room in this treehouse three flights up people
    keep coming in
They ring the buzzer in various codes which we often ignore
You can tell by the pressure applied to the button who it is anyway
They keep coming in I won't enumerate but they're all there at all
    of the ages and stages we
Were it's too crowded isn't it or not you love it whoever but I'm
    pushed far inside
At this moment finding space down the well of myself
Though I am this land this apartment in hieroglyphs inscribed round
    the well as I drift down

This apartment wasn't me really it was everyone else it was the
    outer world
How did it all fit in it was all-nighters parties near-fistfights
    breakdowns
Endless conversation and controversy dinner parties on a bed
An eternal heart-to-heart "It smells like McSorley's in here"
A death occurs and a couple more offstage the room's full of mourners
    I sit up half the night
Staring near the shoehorn hanging from a nail staring at nothing
Some wood in a bookshelf that never got varnished
Trying to understand how a person vanishes will I ever vanish

Outside's the block one year I dreamed so much I wasn't sure I could
    tell the difference
Between sleeping and waking the block became me full of symbols
People keyed into my problems speaking somewhat in my codes but
Later the block became itself again
So fixedly that it's difficult for me to see it though it changes
Gets restaurants shops yuppies punks speculators drifting types
Buildings and cars and trash cans still there
Same old people whom I do like fixed in place just like me

So I walk up the block trapped in time not even so much in those
    times
But the time of walking up the block and around it to the store
Over the years I had too often walked on that block to the store and back
What do you do in life go to the store and the next day and the next and
Trapped in the time of walking to the store
And back one day I popped free from time
I popped out of sequence out of walking that stretch for a second
    everything felt light I wasn't there
That wasn't the first time something like this had happened
It had happened a few years earlier on Third Avenue
I didn't exactly leave time that time time slowed
And people slowed and walked in slow motion and had naked faces
They all looked vulnerable benign not hard but this time in
    1991
I realized I wasn't even there at all I was unlocated untimed

About a year and a half later and there is no connection particularly
    I left New York

If I Didn't Shiver I Wouldn't Be Cold

"Try to follow your own mind out
and anywhere"
past the stormtroopers on the ice
till I come to the soughtafter
five at the mortuary four on the floor
how many dead by the time I
actually get to the door
through which might be the soughtafter
the soughtafter must be wintry I'm still
on ice no more stormtroopers cold night
stay in the poem—skating
down the white river, now a
breakup of ice god that's pleasurable
or dangerous a melting, coming apart in floes
people on other floes   poets I was younger with
separate and floating too, Ted has a floe
Anne has one Steve Bernadette the separateness
of our situations here is a
manifestation of the universe's cold gold fairness
no one has more to face than this?
and I'm all alone now, I've floated off on
a sidestream or is it the mainstream it's
very wide and my floe is still holding

where is the soughtafter
caresses the icy needles of pines on the banks
my fur coat's white dusted
new snow new coldness
it might be the soughtafter being here
so alone and cold like a mind
a certain mind not thinking
not thinking and not thinking
floating far from my "group"

who are you ice who are you storm
who is this ice I've been for so long
This is distinction, says a voice,
Your features are etched in
ice so everyone can see them

In Needles and to Poet What Are Real Things

Inside crystal walls of my body
Sit in a cold December projecting
Self around streets of old town
Crowd of memories and memories of dreams
Alfred's Jeweler's was really *there* but in my dream of
When? was doors down, part of that dark bar (The Rails?
not The Couple Up)
Across from the real railroad tracks and down from
       the Harvey House
No difference between real and dreamed now
Eileen and Eula see me off on a
Train, I think in a dream.

And words? So what.

I own no jewels from Alfred's but an
Opal from Glen's is cracked.
Any event in a life will do, or dream, such an object
       resonates. And
Word—just a word doesn't go.
I put down some any words but they don't
Go viz '-pathic musical quarters. Aren't your
Language dusks smoky making feeble trays of vision?'
I could say anything—frozen jockstrap
In my smart mouth, but why?

The trellis of words collapses. The Now
Collapses, it's of no interest, the
Thing being said is Stupid, like a Sponge
It soaks up the present's secondhand ideas
All those fuzzy words. Only the past is true
       as it changes
I walk into Claypool's real or a dream
Oranges, there's the tattooed pale
Mohave woman in a scarf, and

Pepe behind the butcher's counter—1950.
An interesting area of groceries, off to the left
Is riskier, farther, more complex in the dream of it
The future's there having happened
Telling me that possible stories
Of me in the world of success or failure
Cause rearrangements of the bins, their cans of yams shifting
I'm frightened I'll lose not my I, but yours in me

Which I do.
After the first death there are no words for this loss
Only a different dream and not in your eyes
Where am I going not far from the Newbre Mortuary
Or there back to alley house discover I must live
In filth black dust crumbling toys
If I am to appreciate your poetry and give you an A
Your words for what's precious, which you say
Is ours, and give you my A.

1992

It's dark down the rue Caulaincourt
where I don't want to be in a red silk shirt
when we first ate at Au Pierre de la Butte
five years ago this wasn't my city
it was us not unmoored I'm walking with you
it's raining we're wet down the hill down some steps

towards the bridge over Montmartre Cemetery
over history dead great men unlike me
I've always wanted to be a
dead great man though not exactly dead but
I'll never make it
partly because not a man
partly because this is no world for greats
anyone's buried under dross of so many
made prominent by technology's pomp
of produce its certifying empire
I have a dream of staying at that Hotel Ibis
I want to lie in its sterile Americanized arms

what was I, fear to be no one here
you aren't you and I'm not I
but that's why I came here to see how I'd change—
implies that "I" sees and registers the change, unchanged—
haven't youth now, with which to conquer a few
have only a tradition in poetry
bound up in me which who wants in a world
where all art's patently successful
ratified by treaty packaged by conglomerate celebrated
by comment and dropped to consider real business:

prizes, photos, advances, GATT Business English the MLA
the Booker Prize Oxford Cambridge the New York Publishing
Houses Pulitzer MacArthur the Dorothea Tanning Award
administered by the Academy of American Poets the Penguin

Poets the Bloodaxe Poets the New Directions Poets NAFTA the new
CIA the Market the Stock Exchange

empty
as I am except for my self who observes me
both lovingly and detachedly, and my tradition:
I'll make a poem for you which holds locked up a living voice -
the key's on your own tongue—
I'll teach you some things about Berrigan Padgett
Kyger Thomas Oliver Riley or how to
win a poetry prize given out by yourself
but that's not the ending it's walking
in a wet Parisian dark that's
utilizable, every inch, even used up

New Dreams

Back in my dreams which aren't far away
The bakery downstairs approximately
Is a dress store   Peggy sees me onto
A sleeper on a train bound for Italy
Night before last in China before the revolution
You tried to send me back to Boston
But I wanted to stay here in China despite
Its future population problem
"I'll figure out a way to stay"
Standing in a store of traditional instruments

What dress am I buying a pink one No
This store used to be on St. Mark's Place
Too-thin dresses made out of scarves
In Paris my history's the desert
They won't let me speak unless I'm young
In a dress and say nothing much
No one, and what would I say
Alexander Dumas Père has died
And I was just speaking to his head
Disconnected statuary now it's dead

I saw myself with six lines on my face
"Weil" means Bridge or To Suffer, do I
Holy Men naked parade by, I'm tired of them
Don't say that again   Going to my clinic,
At night in the gutter, I carry
A dilapidated begonia, older
We're French women "going to the doctor"
I write down "Nothing 'French' happened yesterday"
In another dream I'm described:
"She has orgasms eats sleeps writes"

In Paris history's the desert
Each form we've made beautiful and dry

Not as story it sits there defying your judgment
"I was once made by people now am not"
Tempestuous outside again. high-
Heeled footsteps in wind
A bus in sunlight; air of computers
Invisible thread snood with sparklets
I wonder if I have been born
If you deny time's young you'll be hurt

47th Birthday

Exactly the color
of a gray tear the sky is still
trees a torn yellow color and black
leftover dahlias maybe or mums not to look at
Inside there
is the delicate frame of a three-month-old fetus
perlite skeletons of Siamese twins
inside there the meek dead and deformed
have been adequately investigated.

I have a self in my own hollow face
a seeing that floats within my bones
a tear of mine more untrappable than organ or femur
a thinking, perceiving tear

Walk of no nationality in this instant
though the trees look French they aren't French
though I look American I'm animal and tear
I'm gray cloud November speak nothing today
think in English nothing familiar, no familiar thoughts in France.

This is an experiment, Monsieur Buffon,
in whether or not I'm yours or anyone's or my old idea of myself
the answer is I am not, I've thrown those away

Enter the Ménagerie of the Jardin des Plantes, for the first time
25 francs, no people too cold and gray, no animal moves today
in the brilliance of yellow and the elegance
the sensuous requiem of gray, I'm shown the souls of animals
with me, into me, not moving no sound.
These are my first real owls, they know me for eyes and a form
the sika knows me, the llama knows me
for a form in a black matte coat, my big eyes empty with
the colors of this park, myself saying to these others
we're like god exalted but we're dead, we're god-on-earth destroyed.

Provincial, silly earth. This my new problem
not wanting to countenance with my eyes like any other animal's
our worldwide city
I want to be dead but not as our technological life is dead
I want to be dead in a thoughtless presence, a topaz presence
like an animal's eye.

Bobby (First Visit Back to the States)

Locust locket tule-fuzz locket: First—
lobule of memory expand—I'm oh
sixteen night with tule-dust blown, riding
with Bobby Tony Greg Listen KOMA
static fuzz from Oklahoma City
Damp dust-smelling wind means sprinkling of rain
That's all we ever get but it's
a sweet change a stirring, on the east end
of town by Wetmore's where Bobby later
lives, but first, something else, I'm smoking
grass in my twenties projected back to exact
instant in car black air smell the wind white fleck
That instant has a name: grace between what happens
catch it now a pale building passage of
Paris light but next there's Bobby
over a year ago haven't seen him in years
Vietnam like everyone bad alcoholism
recovery now dying of cancer in lungs
I've missed the drama first he's eighteen now he's now
we sit outside—there's the darkening river
he itemizes fates in our high school class
"For me the good feeling in my life is
connected with that class," he says, and
"The Indians all say that our class was
the marker, first time they felt part of the school"
Class of '63, "I'm afraid I did too much drinking
over in the Indian Village," then,
"I'm looking forward if that's there
to seeing Greg and Tony when I die"
Tony dead since '68—"His death's still
sharp for everyone" —Greg more recently,
heart attack, was the one I secretly loved
I admit that and make Bobby say Greg was gay
"Not quite comfortable with it," he says
"I wanted to hear somebody say it," I say

Bobby says, "He always fell for young
Mexican guys, personally I think they were Tony"
well I don't think so myself, Tony
was everyone's friend, simply, being
even-tempered and intelligent also handsome
getting blown up in Nam stopped him changing
Poem's too clear river's dark sky big
"Did you ever hear about the albino beaver," I say,
"Greg and I saw, one night in the river· no one
believed us my father just laughed" "You should
talk to the Mohaves about that stuff"
Tells me the story of Bear McCord's father
Bear—a Mohave—comes home one day and
says to his mother and aunt I saw a white owl
they both start crying and say Your father
will die in three days and so he does
"What do you think happens," Bobby asks,
"after I die? David Andes was here, and said as a
scientist, he can't believe there's anything"
I say, "I think we already know what death's like
there are moments in life when we're dead   "
I mean like that car-riding river-wind moment
"Death's good," I say, and am infused with
incipient terror as intensity
we are just about exactly the river
thick and purple eddy-lined under stars

In the Basement of Claypool's Department Store

The angers closest to my heart
objectify
and formal child's back—
my old haunt
basement where I
don't have to be a pro
On the shelves of this store
marbles and grooves
the honesty toys
Other end's for death
I've stood over there
rearranging my
blood
red steel and glass so
vowel sounds could cope
Rectum, scented, is here with its
reminders of
pea-jacket deaths and requitals
Girls need a peignoir to die
My dad asked my mom for his pea jacket
I was standing there
picking out a toy
a pink poem that looked like a
gas station
You know I didn't or did I
want to
undertake property research viz
this poetry's
ascribed and reputable so
a woman can finally be something
On the walls I see portraits of smart us
likeness of lamellibranch
slime minds
opening a fraction so you can lick them
The luminescence of my anger

still keeps me in thrall
I count prizewinning boyscout poems
by girls and boys
avantgardist or quaint
I have poison tears forty-eight
Of and move, of and move
The human body is the most foolish
invention of these
times
Gray light encircles the store
Pick up one more toy
to look at
not the body toy
with its diamonds and groin
rose cunt flesh pretty
the brain lungs the liver etc   no
the body's not the last
toy in the store
it's that plain one it's flat
count it, be smart
Shake it and count
One one one
One for the genius
the President of Poetry one for
the logic of
philosopher or pauper
one even one
for the girl
I'll take it and find out there's
one
There's only one toy in this disease
pound it or strike it caress it
one one one

Going Back Mornings

I don't have to live I'm not even four and I don't think of it

Up at the army barracks our postwar housing and facing down the gully to the river beloved and better than any future promise of yours

Old young the same and it's Needles I love over there's Lily Hill a silvery green color arrows up within the white of "the desert lily" better than my life

Back I'm back to no life yet at pre-four look at myself from outside it's me or one of my babies in corduroy pants running with round butt hurrying

To the edge of the rocks dirt gully why is it so finite down there everything's so finite even murder would be I'm not but what we do is and what we see

I want something to give to the infinite only myself is what I have I don't have to be anywhere oh but the river valley's all beauty before the dredge on a boat to a sandbar a Mohave stands way out in shoals to catch a carp with his hands they know how to eat them even with the bones we've stopped we're here our beer and water-melon stay cold in the water

We let such reality slip away because if we pretend we are no longer animals but creatures who have invented and we have our own intellects made our own finity which can be subdivided into infinite parts to rearrange why that's infinity enough and we can construct and manage our own awards and rewards out of our notions of what we want

Our notions speak to me in Paris near fifty tug at my false heart of movie feelings saying don't go back to your childhood that's too dangerous for our world which wants as many thoughts as many words as you have of it as it is now just to prove that it's alive

I don't want to be alive is a flame poppy alive I'm being like that

But I can't hold onto it there are my shoes I have to go walk to the store and night already waits for today because time will be passed in the usual way obliterating my love which is nature in time we more and more obliterate that love

Place Blanche

I've been left with myself here

finding a voice by accident the same one careless or careful

in this pronoun come into its other room (a country or
      language might be there)

the wind that blows the tree outside like a flag a green rag
      whose icon is a woman upsidedown

and one comes up the street cold past the sexshops the photos
      of tits and cunts with black band-aids or
      chickenflesh shaved Le Parfum de Mathilde is pussy

so think of that as far as the newsstand read the Herald Tribune
      our fathers are in power in the States and some
      exactly my age

of course I want my poems to be different from my older
      ones and from yours

because I'm not you though I'm fatherlike too but I want my
      self so it will flow into my deeper
      self it's the only path down

and if I "sound like me" that may be as meaningless
      as that the new government presents my own father's
      sentiments as revolution a word sold for attention
      and so belonging in the sex parlor I've just passed:
      where you the Speaker of the House spread your legs

but really I tell the literal hill of Montmartre up which I
      walk   as it opens to me from the inside dreaming

to speak as I hill not so much as I house that white-walled
apartment on a woundup street but as the scary land
beneath the thin floors that keep us from it as our
thin words like "revolution" keep us from revolution

this the hill where St. Denis brought his head all the
way from St. Denis carrying it as in my poem the First
Woman carried her head below the earth but he ascended
instead and then he really died

I live on with a fragile necklace of demarcation around my
neck between the world the irrational above and
the vast rationality beneath hidden within me

More Below a Dream Of

Doug and I splash in fresh water naked a
lake under rock
our hair is damp you can see
the wavering columns of our bodies so the water
is clear clean next to clean smell of wet stone

It's an old lake this dream
under a rock eave we look out to sea of a large lake
without a far shore
a beach now we walk on still naked
and sit under trees

Idyll, of course
This part of one goes out to other one, too
a passing ship, very far and dark, a deathy notice
wet sand on legs and ass
lie back and look up at green and blue lace
éclat of light in small bursts through

Of course we aren't really like this what are we
like not exquisitely realized in the present as
the present, and this is a waking dream
my parallel present
not jewels of thought but unthought
emerald continuum Doug says,

"there two together because that proves it"
I start to ask what but forget
and forgetting is a pleasure not an irritant

are we here despite the misery of others? but
anyone might be *here*
they begin to appear along the shore
and I become a vantage-point watching us all
rising higher and higher above Doug and myself

Remember What I Came Here to Do
to This World Very Little Actually

I came here so that the
I came to be equal in surprise to
I came empty-handed before being dried
I am a poisonous epoch
I was at four a shape of love and reason
I was at fifteen capable of heinous pity
I'm not so foolish as to
I think at 34 that I know who the best poets are
I saw your footage of what you said was the age
I meet 6000 men and 15 women on the way to
I thought we would have more influence on
I perform no generous act '84
I put self back in the genie bottle for the fad
I, and did I ever love
I, loving truth more than myself, am abased by
I was poor but never poor enough
I have as much authority to speak as
I was against all war and loved mostly soldiers
I have no identity I recognize except in myself
I go in there it's the page of a book I rip it
I am infidel to country
I, guilty always through speaking, inhale
I, that year, hating the species, thought of myself as inhuman
I think the imagination is more real than
I, I said, presume we're all fully responsible for
I once visited their great graves that was years ago
I measured that year in sequence of vivid dreams of it
I was once the shaman of a death
I keep trying to be honest in this glittering wind
I find you difficult like as not
I saw it and I said
I will never be complete without the
I caressed him too clumsily
I borrow someone else's form what else is a body

Office

Office is
love, metric love's
practice
By which I mean
not with a swollen foot bare
like X's in
my funny dream—and
had tied a red string
around his
foot!

Back
in the vicinity
of the A house
is where my true office is—
love
is the substance I am most
which releases
me not from
the body
but from its en-
culturation
as senses sights signification
Love, oval, valid
make the word change
so you can see it
so I can show you the word love change it
to silver—
it's in the "dining room"
of the alley house
a torn silver layer
peeling from air's
venal
navel

———

If we could free
this love
our feet would be light
the motel walls
out the window
float
and change from
gray to silver
everything's silvered now in
my gaze

I suppose I couldn't
function as function—
what do you want me to do?
Not float up? why?
(I've never understood you)
house darkens
dark silver draws closer
together
empty
around me
rose tightens
in here
if you lose self
and then relaxes
I mean its grip

Mysteries of Small Houses

Poverty much maligned but beautiful
has resulted in smaller houses replete with mysteries
How can something so finite
so petite and shallow have
the infinite center I sense there? There

in the alley house for example
I enter it again, utterly still in the morning and with
shadows around its door mouth and throughout
frontroom bedroom diningroom kitchen room of washtubs and
porch made my room, all
small, small and worn linoleum blue pattern pink
flowers, but now it's all shadows
'cause inside its center I'm, or is it we're
It's I'm that I won't ever know
completely unless I do when I die

How

do

we manage to base ourselves on dark ignorance so
house of pressed-down pushed-in
origin, is such poverty; or
apartments where people die, again the strange dense
center of the four tiny rooms on St. Mark's Place may be that
Ted died there and so left a mystery vortex inside that fragile
apartment on stilts —Doug, do you think so?

you

lived there. This apartment where we are now isn't
so poor, though it's small
The house must be small and fragile
My grandparents' house too had four small rooms
and no bath or shower and whenever you sat on the
toilet a mynah bird across the lot cried out
Their house had a darkness where they slept

I know I'm not talking about poverty exactly but not
having, why have it's such
an illusion, and the body-self such a shadowy fragile house —

Go in and find that room that secret
is it under it   or inside, it's inside a shadow
if I could just slip into it— and if I do I'm still whole but
mum in old Needles
the motel's too big the churches are too and the mute
low-lying schools
there's the desert beyond them that I try to keep housed from
no thin flesh there no coursing fluid no thought

Lady Poverty

Sings in the gullies
To all you go without is added more as the years
Youth's face health certain friends then more and
so to get poorer
life's arrow—tapers thinner sharper

She always sang there to purify
not the desert always pure
but me of my corrupt furor
So losing more further along in this dream of
firstrate firmament fireworks—
consigned to roam above brown dirt occasional
maxilla, and be shaped badly—
twisted internally· join her truly

She's I

She should be

the shape of a life is impoverishment—what
can that mean
except that loss is both beauty and knowledge—
has no face no eyes for
seasons of future delivery—rake the dirt
like Mrs. Miller used to
down at the corner had a desert yard and raked her dirt.

Beginning in poverty as a baby there is nothing
for one but another's food and warmth
should there ever be more
than a sort of leaning against and trust a food for
another from out of one—that would be
· poverty—we're taught not to count on
anyone, to be rich,

youthful, empowered
but now I seem to know that the name of a self is poverty
that the pronoun I means such and that starting so
poorly, I can live

Susan Cataldo, 1992

About the Author

Alice Notley was born in Bisbee, Arizona, on November 8, 1945, and grew up in Needles, California. She was educated at Barnard College and at The Writers Workshop, University of Iowa, receiving the appropriate degrees. During the late sixties and early seventies she lived a peripatetic, rather outlawish poet's life (San Francisco, Bolinas, London, Essex, Chicago) before settling on New York's Lower East Side. For sixteen years there, she was an important force in the eclectic second generation of the so-called New York School of poetry. She has never tried to be anything but a poet, and all her ancillary activities have been directed to that end. She is the author of more than twenty books of poetry, including *At Night the States*, the double volume *Close to Me and Closer (The Language of Heaven)* and *Désamère*, and *How Spring Comes*, which was a winner of the San Francisco Poetry Award. Her *Selected Poems* was published in 1993. Her book-length poem *The Descent of Alette* was published by Penguin in 1996. She is a two-time NEA grant recipient and the recipient of a General Electric Foundation Award, a NYFA fellowship, several awards from The Fund for Poetry, and a grant from the Foundation for Contemporary Performance Arts, Inc. She now lives permanently in Paris.

PENGUIN POETS

Paul Beatty	*Joker, Joker, Deuce*
Ted Berrigan	*Selected Poems*
Philip Booth	*Pairs*
Jim Carroll	*Fear of Dreaming*
Nicholas Christopher	*5° & Other Poems*
Carl Dennis	*Ranking the Wishes*
Diane di Prima	*Loba*
Stuart Dischell	*Evenings and Avenues*
Stephen Dobyns	*Common Carnage*
Paul Durcan	*A Snail in My Prime*
Amy Gerstler	*Crown of Weeds*
Amy Gerstler	*Nerve Storm*
Debora Greger	*Desert Fathers, Uranium Daughters*
Robert Hunter	*Glass Lunch*
Robert Hunter	*Sentinel*
Barbara Jordan	*Trace Elements*
Jack Kerouac	*Book of Blues*
Ann Lauterbach	*And For Example*
Ann Lauterbach	*On a Stair*
William Logan	*Vain Empires*
Derek Mahon	*Selected Poems*
Michael McClure	*Three Poems*
Carol Muske	*An Octave Above Thunder*
Alice Notley	*The Descent of Alette*
Alice Notley	*Mysteries of Small Houses*
Anne Waldman	*Kill or Cure*
Robert Wrigley	*In the Bank of Beautiful Sins*

Printed in the United States
by Baker & Taylor Publisher Services